CHARLES KELLY is one of the original mountain bikers. With his friend Gary Fisher, he invented the new breed of bike that has turned off-road riding into a recreational activity for millions worldwide.

His first bikes were assembled from frames rescued from local scrapheaps. The bikes were tested to destruction and the results put back together. Word soon got round and Charlie helped start the first commercial mountain bike company. In 1980 he founded *The Fat Tire Flyer*, the first off-road magazine. In 1983, to avoid any conflict between his writing and the bike business, Charlie ended his connections with Fisher Mountainbikes. Today he is editor of *Mountain Bike for the Adventurer* magazine. He lives in Fairfax, California, with his wife Mary, a dog named Amelia and several bicycles.

NICK CRANE is one of Britain's leading bicycle adventurers. He has ridden a mountain bike up Kilimanjaro, Africa's highest mountain, through the Gobi Desert to the point on the earth most remote from the sea and traversed Snowdonia's fourteen peaks by mountain bike in under 24 hours. He is a regular contributor to *World* magazine and is the author of several books on cycle touring. On those infrequent occasions when he's not travelling, he parks his backpack in London.

# RICHARD'S
# Mountain Bike Book

## by Charles Kelly and Nick Crane

**Pan Books**
London, Sydney and Auckland

**This book is dedicated to all the
English teachers who wondered
what I was thinking about.**
—*Charles Kelly*

Some of the material for this book has appeared previously, and I would like to mention and thank those who gave me the original opportunity to publish it.

Portions of the Repack story appeared in *Bicycling*, January 1979.

Portions of 'Riding Technique' appeared in *Cyclist*, August 1984.

Portions of 'The Arctic Cycle' appeared in *Cyclist*, February 1986 and *Bicycle Action*, January 1986.

Portions of other chapters have appeared in *Fat Tire Flyer*, various issues.

**Photographic credits**

Pages, 20, 24, 28 Wende Cragg; 32, (top) Wende Cragg, (bottom) Fisher MountainBikes; 33, Fisher MountainBikes; 36, Charles Kelly; 40, Point Reyes Bikes; 44-45, 48, Wende Cragg; 52, Charles Kelly; 56, Wende Cragg; 58-59, J. Ribol; 64, Fisher MountainBikes; 70, 72, 74, Charles Kelly; 77, Tim Leighton-Boyce; 78, Charles Kelly; 81, 84-85, Charles Kelly; 88, Fisher MountainBikes; 91, Tim Leighton-Boyce; 93, Cannondale Corporation; 96, Muddy Fox; 100, Richard Grant; 104, Fisher MountainBikes; 106, Paul Willis; 108, 109, Tim Leighton-Boyce; 112, Penny Stron; 115, Nick Crane; 118, Tim Gartside; 120, 123, Charles Kelly; 126, Peter Inglis; 130, HKP; 132, Richard Grant; 134, Richard Ballantine; 136, Charles Kelly; 138, Richard Ballantine; 142, HKP; 154, Tim Gartside; 156 Tim Gartside/Peter Murphy; 160, Peter Inglis; 168, Adrian Crane; 173, Nick Crane; 176, Caroline Forbes; 180, 181, Peter Inglis; 182, 184, Nick Crane.

First published in Great Britain 1988 by Oxford Illustrated Press

This edition published 1990 by Pan Books Ltd, Cavaye Place, London SW10 9PG.

9 8 7 6 5 4 3 2 1

Copyright © Richard's Bicycle Books Ltd., 1989.

ISBN 0 330 31302 9

Printed and bound in Great Britain by Richard Clay Ltd, Bungay, Suffolk

Series created by Richard Grant and Richard Ballantine

Designed by Richard Grant

Produced by Tamshield Limited, London.

# Contents

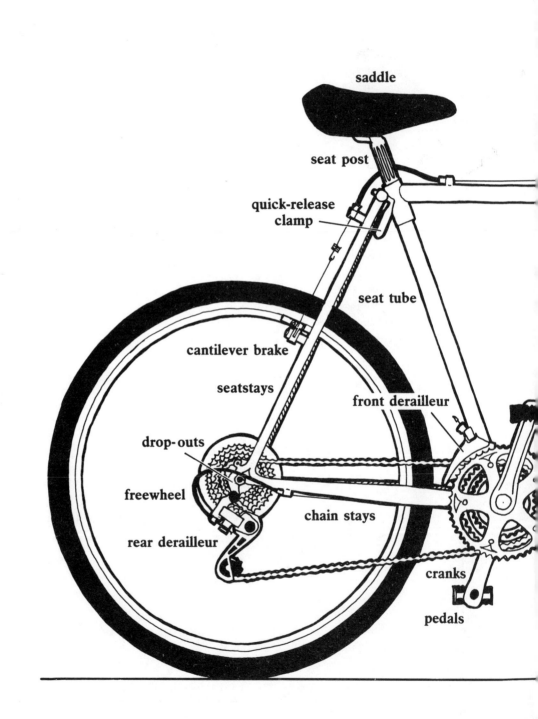

saddle

seat post

quick-release
clamp

seat tube

cantilever brake

seatstays

front derailleur

drop-outs

freewheel

chain stays

rear derailleur

cranks

pedals

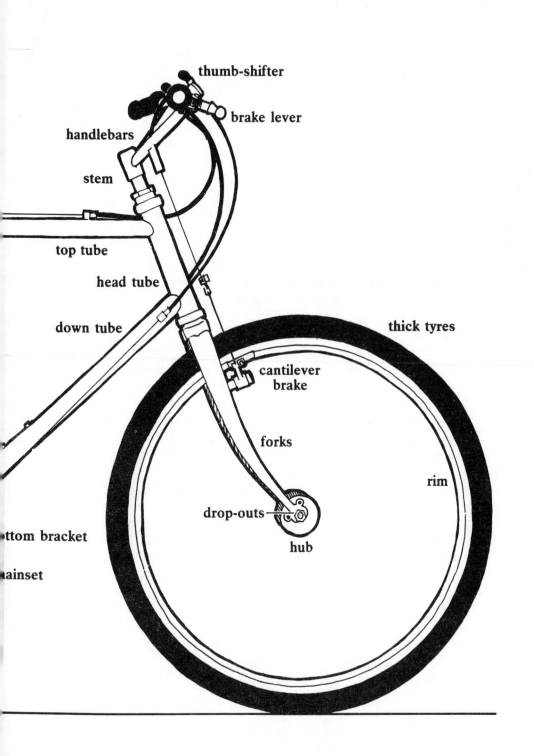

thumb-shifter

brake lever

handlebars

stem

top tube

head tube

down tube

thick tyres

cantilever
brake

forks

rim

drop-outs

hub

ttom bracket

ainset

# Background

Mountain bikes, or ATBs (All-Terrain Bicycles), have had more impact on the bicycle industry in the 1980s than any other innovation. The breakthrough came in the late seventies when the fat tyres common on American bicycles 50 years ago were coupled with the bicycle and materials technology of the eighties; the result is a bicycle that can travel on nearly any terrain.

At first confined to a small group of northern California recreational users who built their own bikes, mountain bikes appeared on the mass market in the USA in 1981, in the UK in 1984, and since that time they have spread to all parts of the cycling community. For several years the growth curve for mountain bike sales has remained at nearly 100 per cent, doubling the number of riders each year.

Mountain bikes are being used in all aspects of cycling. Touring cyclists have adopted them for use in the most remote areas ever to see bicycles; mountain bikers have toured the Arctic, the Himalayas, and the Andes, and have conquered the highest peaks in Europe and Africa, Mont Blanc and Kilimanjaro.

Competitive riders have established a racing circuit, and national mountain bike championships have been held in the United States since 1983. The first organized mountain bike events in the UK were held in 1984. The growth of the sport worldwide has inspired national mountain bike organizations in many countries and the first World Championships were hosted by France in 1987. Mountain bike competition has already spawned an offshoot called Observed Trials, which has taken off on its own.

But aside from the competitive or touring aspects, mountain bikes are just plain fun for riders of any level of experience, and most owners spend a majority of their riding time on ordinary roads. The rugged construction coupled with agility and performance make mountain bikes the practical choice for every type of cycling except road racing.

# Foreword

The correct and conventional way to preface a book about the mountain bike is to explain in simple terms what a mountain bike is, who it's for, why it is monumentally significant, and why this book's authors are more eminently qualified than any others to write about mountain bikes. But that is to treat the mountain bike as if it were just another piece of bicycle hardware, and you, the browsing reader, someone in need of just another handbook.

This book is something more: it is both a handbook and a chronicle of a dream. All the essential handbook elements—the anatomy of the bike; the naming of parts; the tips on riding techniques; on thin air repairs, on how expeditions go from idea to execution—are contained within its pages. But as anyone who has ridden, or even dreamed of riding a mountain bike knows, the machine is considerably more than the sum of its parts. It represents a dream turned into reality: the dream of going more or less anywhere off-road, whether it's just the local forest fire road or all the way to the top of the mountain. This book is about that dream, the dreamers who made it happen, the revolution the mountain bike has realised, and some of the adventures it has made possible.

The genesis of this book goes back to 1977. I was a reporter travelling around northern California on the lookout for offbeat stories. An acquaintance suggested that I check out Fairfax, a small rural town in Marin County north of San Francisco, where there was a local bicycle phenomenon known as clunkers. In Fairfax's only bike shop, the owner, on hearing my English accent, enthusiastically engaged me in a long conversation about a British lightweight framebuilder he much admired. Since he did most of the talking, and I didn't have the heart to confess that my interest in bikes had ended in childhood when my tricycle was stolen, I waited for a suitable gap in the conversation to ask about clunkers. When I did, his face fell. They were, he indicated, the scourge of the earth and he was having no truck with them. It was a foretaste of the fear and loathing with which the conventional cycling business would eventually greet mountain bikes, as clunkers were later christened.

Fortunately the shop owner's natural American hospitality got the better of his hostility towards clunkers and he introduced me to Gary Fisher, then his part-time workshop mechanic. Gary, already used to the passions his homebrew clunkers could arouse, signalled that we should meet later. That evening we met with his partner Charlie Kelly. Their HQ and Gary's home was a rundown one-room shack in a back alley behind the town bar. Its thin wooden walls were decorated with beat-up cycle frames and bike race posters. The coffee table was a sheet of ply supported by empty six-packs. Every few minutes, or so it seemed, a newcomer, his jeans and T-shirt covered in sweat and dust from some particularly hair-raising off-road ride, would pile into the tiny room—bike and all—and discuss how to fix some part on his clunker or improve its performance.

Gary and Charlie were the unofficial leaders of a pack of hardcore hippie bike bums who got their rush riding hard off-road. In the sixties they had been in San Francisco, doing some of their growing up in the psychedilic world of Haight-Ashbury, Gary running his own light show, Charlie, five years older, as roadie to a local rock 'n' roll band, The Sons of Champlin. Like many in the seventies, Gary and Charlie had moved out of the city, north into rural Marin, where they first met, to live less frenetic, more laid-back lives. The head badge on their clunkers sported the Hells Angels death's head legend 'Ride to Live, Live to Ride'. Their invention, the clunker, was just the means to that end. It didn't look like a bike, more like a motorbike without an engine.

Since I knew nothing about bikes and they talked ten to the dozen, a ride was arranged. I was completely unfit, overweight, with a pack-a-day habit, and only just emerging from the dangerous oblivion that comes from researching too closely an article about Marin's other budding homegrown industry, cannabis farming. Gary and Charlie, by contrast, were blindingly fit. They rode every day. Gary was a national class cyclo-cross competitor. Charlie still made his living moving pianos for The Sons of Champlin. When he wasn't riding he was roller-skating or skateboarding.

They loved the challenge of turning someone new on to off-road riding. After two hours hurtling around the Marin hills, shooting down fire roads, I was sold. It was the most fun I had ever had on a bike. Did I want one? Gary had devised 20 or so clunkers out of cannibalised old Schwinn Excelsior frames. Go on—take one back to England. Just $275. Two days later I collected my very own clunker. I was a convert. Even then Gary and Charlie knew they were on to something. They were the free-wheeling alchemists of a very sixties-type dream.

Gary was the mechanic, the inventor, and a test rider. Through cyclo-cross he was on the fringes of the cycle world, but not of it. He knew exactly what sort of heresy he was promoting. Charlie was also a test rider, constantly suggesting improvements, tracking down components, then using them until they broke. He was also the chronicler. Early on, when only a handful of friends rode together, Charlie was noting down and recording their feats. He'd sit for hours crafting the articles, sending them to outdoor magazines, only to have them politely rejected. Who wanted to read about a bunch of escapist hippies haring down a California hillside on junk bicycles? Egged on by Gary, he'd rewrite and resubmit. Slowly he got published. Around Fairfax, Gary and Charlie had turned several hundred on to mountain bikes. The first custom bikes were appearing. Word was spreading. Charlie started the *Fat Tire Flyer*, a newsletter-cum-fanzine that would in time metamorphose into a fully fledged magazine. Its style was Charlie's; underground, wry, dry, and irreverent, detached from commercial hype but deeply attached to the freedom the mountain bike could deliver. The *Flyer* and Charlie, writing as SeeKay, was the authentic voice of a bicycle revolution in the making. Many of the articles and some that preceded the *Flyer* were too good to allow to rot in some backcopies department and now form the basis of this book.

Not everyone loved the *Flyer*. Manufacturers, who were slowly realising that they were going to have to climb aboard the mountain bike bandwagon, were never comfortable with it. Few supported it. The *Flyer* and Charlie kept the record straight, refused to hand out plaudits to phonies just because of the size of their advertising budgets, and was never afraid to call a bike unworthy of the name 'mountain bike', if it was really a cheap, useless klutz rather than believe disingenuous claims about it being a 'low-end, budget-conscious machine'.

Conflict with the bicycle business was never far away. It was not that the mountain bike was disliked by the the smug, closed clubbable world that in the pre-mountain bike era called itself the cycling business. It was positively loathed. It represented, and still does to hardcore traditionalists, a rejection of every one of the premises that underpinned cycling. First it stood on its head the very basis of modern cycling—that the only place to ride was the road. This, in turn, made nonsense of the notion that the lighter the bike, the skinnier its wheels, the better it would go. Kelly and Fisher's solid-as-a-rock mountain bike with its chunky tires and heavy-duty parts was a throwback, a contradiction. It would never catch on, they were repeatedly told by many who now sell more mountain bikes than any other type of bike. Some even threatened to do their damnedest to see that the phenomenon would never catch on. Fortunately, for the millions who can now enjoy riding mountain bikes in places once only accessible by foot or horseback, Gary and Charlie didn't give a damn.

They went into business together to build the first commercial mountain bikes. At the 1981 New York Bicycle Show, Japanese manufacturers, less inhibited about what was 'correct' and ever quick to spot a trend, flocked enthusiastically around one of their first production prototypes. The Japanese liked what they saw, measured up, and went home and cloned mountain bikes. Senior Japanese bike executives started arriving in Marin, demanding to be taken on off-road excursions.

But it still wasn't an easy ride. The partnership between Charlie and Gary was short, ending in a turbulent and friendship-damaging divorce. With the benefit of 20/20 hindsight it was always clear that Gary with his tenacious competitive instinct was the one willing to fight his way through the commercial minefields of fluctuating exchange rates, treacherous suppliers and slow-paying customers in order to get a slice of the industry he created. (In 1988 Fisher Mountainbikes planned to produce 10,000 bikes, creating sales worth over $6 million.)

High-pressure business was never really Charlie's style. He'd come out of the Army in 1968, with no particular ambition, except never to wear a tie again. Smalltime business was okay, tolerable. Helping some bigwig Marin lawyer assemble his hand-built mountain bike in his backyard on a Saturday morning and showing him how to have a good time on it suited the maverick in Charlie. Shipping bikes in boxes in their thousands from Japan and Taiwan didn't. Writing was far more rewarding.

Charlie split from Gary and concentrated on the *Flyer*, hugely enjoying his role as the movement's self-effacing, easy-going apostle, encouraging others to push the mountain bike revolution to new limits.

One of those who hardly needed encouragement was Nick Crane, the author of the expeditions section of this book. He first got wind of mountain bikes in 1979 when he was editor of the London-based *International Cycling Guide*, an annual publication closely studied by bicycle cognoscenti worldwide. In 1982 the Guide nominated the first true production mountain bike, the Fisher-Kelly-Ritchey Montare as its Bike of the Year. Inside the mainstream industry Nick, as editor, was considered nuts, yet another who had pinned his colours to the wrong mast.

Few realised that for Nick the mountain bike was the bicycle he had been waiting to be invented: the perfect adventure and expedition vehicle. He was already pushing the envelope of off-road endurance before the term mountain bike was invented. In 1976 while Kelly and Fisher were racing clunkers down the sun-blessed slopes of Marin's Mount Tamalpais, Nick, 6,000 miles away, was riding and carrying a conventional touring bike to the summit of the Old Man of Coniston, an uninviting, windswept, rock-strewn, 2,631 foot peak in the Lake District.

It was a fairly typical Nick Crane outing; bold, unusual and physically exhausting—all the hallmarks of the sort of expeditions with which the British public now associate the name Crane. Nick and his cousins, Dick and Adrian, specialize in the conquest of extremes. Over the last five years, the Cranes, in various combinations, have run the Himalayas from end to end, raced by foot across the African bush, and run, climbed, and ridden England's three highest peaks within 24 hours.

If Gary and Charlie were the unabashed adventurers of the mountain-bike business then the Cranes were intrepid pioneers of expeditionary odysseys, always on the lookout for the next, strange, exotic challenge. For Nick especially, the coming of the mountain bike was like a hand meeting a glove. It added an extra dimension, new challenges, new adventures became possible. Snowdon's 14 peaks in under 24 hours, the ride up Kilimanjaro, Africa's highest mountain, and the endurance-testing Journey to the Centre of the Earth were knocked off at the rate of one a year between 1984 and 1986. Nobody has done more to prove the mountain bike as the perfect expedition vehicle.

Yet ironically Charlie Kelly and Nick Crane have never met, only corresponded. This book provided a unique opportunity to bring together one of the inventors of the dream and one of the adventurers who has helped to take it to new limits.

Richard Grant
London
1988

## PART ONE: THE MOUNTAIN BIKE
### Charles Kelly

**Charlie Kelly**

# Introduction

There are two broad schools of history. Some think that history is shaped by decisions and actions on the part of individuals. Others believe that the tide of human behaviour is controlled by larger forces, such as population, economic pressures, and the availability of resources.

As a participant in one of the more far-reaching developments in the field of bicycling, a development that is in its own way as significant as the introduction of the chain drive and the 'safety bicycle' to replace the high-wheeled boneshaker, I still speculate on whether a few of my friends and myself really did influence the world, or whether we were just the people who were standing there when the appropriate forces came together. All of us who participated in the seminal mountain bike period of the middle seventies are daily confronted with reminders of our vision and dreams in the form of the mass-produced mountain bike, and still we wonder whether we did anything or whether it just happened to us.

Actually, it was a little bit of both. While the influence of previous pioneers of 'off-road' bicycling cannot be ignored, the development of the technology, but more importantly the marketing of the concept, sprang from a relatively small group of northern Californians, most (but not all) from Marin County. The forces were all there: a good place to ride such bikes, a climate that permitted all-year cycling, a ready supply of bicycle components, and a large contingent of cyclists. At some point in the late seventies the group of at first a few dozen and then a couple of hundred 'clunker' enthusiasts reached a critical mass, and the movement took on a life of its own, independent of any single person's influence or control.

This book is my attempt to set down some of the color and excitement of those days when we thought in our naivete that Joe Breeze's ten prototype mountainbikes were surely enough to satisfy worldwide demand. After all, we thought, who would pay $1,000 for a bike with balloon tyres? To this end I have used some material dating back to the time when no one knew how mountain bikes were going to explode onto the market; the viewpoint of these pieces varies between visionary and naive. I can remember conversations with friends before the first custom mountain bike appeared, where one or another of us would suggest that, 'These clunkers are going to be worth a lot of money someday . . . .'

'Sure,' came the response. 'But how are we going to get any of it?'

For those who are more interested in practical realities rather than romance, this work gives me the opportunity to collect and arrange all the bits of lore and experience that I hope will separate this from all the 'How-To' bicycle books on the stands.

I believe some of the pioneers of the movement deserve a salute that isn't tainted by distance; any number of people who were not there have written accounts purporting to tell the origins of the mountain bike, and they all sound like fiction to me. Some have been given more credit than they deserve, and some have had their accomplishments ignored, depending on who got interviewed in the course of the research. I am not without personal prejudices, but at least this is being written from a first-hand viewpoint.

Charles Kelly
Fairfax, California
1988

## Regarding Language

I try to use language as it was taught to me, and in this respect I am a victim of the sexism inherent in the English language. I hope female readers will forgive me if the anonymous rider is sometimes referred to as 'he'. The alternative is usually a clumsy construction, and I would like to assure female readers that I understand that both sexes are represented among mountain bikers and that any reference to an unnamed 'he' also applies to women.

# Repack

## *1976*

It has been an unseasonably dry winter in northern California, and the three young men are sweating profusely as they push strangely modified bikes up the steep dirt road in the cool air. The subject of their breathless conversation is a detailed analysis of the condition of the road surface, which resembles an excavation site more than it does a road. On occasion one or another will stop and look searchingly back down the hill, perhaps kicking dirt into a small depression or rolling a rock to the side of the road.

These young men belong to the same adrenalin-driven breed that will always be found exploring the limits of human performance; in other circumstances they might be skiing off cliffs, jumping out of aeroplanes, or discovering America. In this instance they have developed their own unique athletic challenge, a race whose participation is limited to a few dozen local residents who know about it and have the unusual cycling equipment necessary to take part. The road they are on is the racecourse.

After more than half an hour of hard work, scrambling and pushing but hardly ever riding their bikes, the trio reaches the crest of the hill, where the road they are on intersects another equally rough dirt road. A small crowd of about fifteen other cyclists, similarly equipped and including a couple of high-energy women, is gathered at the intersection. These people have come up by a slightly easier route that follows a properly surfaced road up part of the hill, but they have also had to ride a couple of miles of steep and rough road to arrive here. The three recent arrivals casually drop their bikes on the road, which has become a jumble of modified machinery.

**Repack start line**

Most of the crowd is in their twenties, but there are a few teenagers and one grizzled individual who claims to be fifty. All are wearing heavy shirts and jeans, and most are also wearing leather gloves and heavy boots. None is wearing a helmet.

Although the scene seems to be chaos, order begins to appear. One of the group takes out of his back pack a well-thumbed notebook and a pair of electronic stopwatches. Moving slowly through the crowd, he begins compiling a list of names. The notebook is the combined scoring system, archives, and publicity for the race, since it contains in addition to today's scoring all the previous race results and the telephone numbers of all the participants. Apparently races are not scheduled, they are spontaneously called together when the sun and moon have assumed appropriate aspects.

As names are taken the note-taker assigns a starting order based on the rider's previous performance and experience. Those racing for the first time are first on the list, followed by those with the slowest previous times. The current course record-holder is accorded the honour of starting last. Now starting times are assigned to the names on the list and a copy of the list is made. The watches are started simultaneously and the note-taker hands one copy of the list and one of the watches to an 'official timer' whose appearance is undistinguished from the rest of the crowd. The timer takes a moment to tape a bottle cap over the reset switch on his watch, then he jumps on his bike and disappears down the hill.

For the next ten minutes the adrenalin content of the air builds while riders attend to their pre-race rituals. Some sit quietly eating oranges, some joke nervously or talk excitedly. Others make minute adjustments to their bikes, adjusting brakes, perhaps letting a little air out of the tyres, or repeatedly shifting the gears, still undecided about which ratio to use for the start.

After an interval that is too short for some and too long for others the first name on the list is called. Up to the line steps a nervous young man who has by now tried every one of his gears without making a decision. He tries a few more last-second shifts as he rolls his bike to the line, which is a rough scratch inscribed in the road surface by the heel of the starter's boot. This is his first race, and he spends his last few seconds at the top of the hill asking questions about the course faster than anyone can answer, although answers are immaterial because he isn't listening anyway.

The starter props the young man up by holding his rear wheel, and as the rider stands on his pedals his legs are quivering. The starter intones, 'Ten seconds . . . five . . . ' Anticipating the start, the rider tries to explode off the line a second before the starter says, 'Go!' But the starter is used to this and he has a firm grip on the wheel, which he releases as he gives the signal. Thrown completely off-balance and draped over the handlebars by his premature jump, the novice wobbles off the line for a few yards before finding the throttle and accelerating to the top of a small rise 100 yards off and then disappearing from sight.

The sport going on here is so unusual and possibly even dangerous that it is unlikely to catch on with the public as a Sunday recreation, but the participants couldn't care less. They are here to thrill themselves, not a distant crowd, and in that respect this is a pure form of athletic endeavour untainted by any commercial connection.

The bicycles in use are as unique as the sport. They are all old balloon-tyre frames dating from the thirties to the fifties; most of them were built by the Schwinn Company but a few other rugged and otherwise extinct species are represented. The standard set of modifications includes the addition of derailleur gearing systems (either 5-speed or 10-speed), front and rear drum brakes, motorcycle brake levers, wide motocross handlebars, handlebar-mounted shift levers, and the biggest knobby bicycle tyres available mounted on heavy Schwinn S-2 steel rims. A few reactionaries cling to their 1- or 2-speed coaster brake models, but the majority have drum brakes and gears, and this looks to be the wave of the future.

The riders affectionately refer to their machines as 'Clunkers', 'Bombers', or 'Cruisers', depending on the owner's local affiliation, and there are not more than 200 of the advanced models in Northern California.

Certainly people have been riding old bikes on dirt roads in all parts of the world as long as there have been old bikes. These Northern California riders have successfully crossed old news-boy-type bikes with the modern '10-speed', and the result is a hybrid that is perfectly adapted to the fire roads and trails of the Northern California hills. In the process of field testing their modifications the researchers have shattered every part to be found on a bicycle. Rims, hubs, handlebars, cranksets, seat posts, saddles, gears, chains, derailleurs, stems, pedals, and frames have all been ground to fragments along with some exterior portions of a number of clunking enthusiasts, who apparently will make any sacrifice in the name of science.

During the early experimental stage some riders recognised the steep dirt road now known as Repack as an ultimate field test for both bike and rider. This rarely used fire road loses 1,300 feet of elevation in less than 2 miles. In addition to its steepness, it features off-camber blind corners, deep erosion ruts, and a liberal sprinkling of fist-sized rocks. The name 'Repack' stems from the coaster-brake era; after a fast trip down the hill the rider would heat the brakes to the point where all the grease in the hub turned to smoke, and it was time to repack the hub.

To the uneducated eye, clunkers might resemble lightweight dirt motorcycles, with their wide handlebars bristling with levers and control cables. The similarity is only visual, however, and cornering on a clunker at high speed is a unique form of body art. A motorcycle has larger tyres, and more important, it has shock absorbers; a clunker is not so equipped, and it tends to become airborne when it hits even slight irregularities in the road surface. In a hard corner a clunker does not have the instant acceleration that a motorcycle rider uses to bring the rear end around, and without shock absorbers the bike skitters. Still, an expert rider can take a clunker around curves much faster than seems possible. Interestingly, photographs taken during Repack races show that the fastest riders raise the least dust.

The absence of shock absorbers on a bicycle can sometimes make hanging onto the clunker handlebars difficult at high speed on a rough surface. Most of the road shock is transmitted directly to the hands, making delicate braking operations difficult. Perhaps the most noticeable feeling (other than relief) at the end of a fast run down Repack is the cramp in the hands caused by this abuse. Here the coaster brake reactionaries claim superiority, since their brakes are foot-operated.

The styles developed and displayed by the expert riders vary with the personalities involved. Joe is known as the 'Mad Scientist.' He has drawn detailed maps of the course which he uses for home study. On race day he walks slowly up the course to inspect it for new hazards, then he rides with a controlled fury that belies his otherwise quiet personality.

A rider named George occupies the other end of the stylistic spectrum, and he has earned the nickname the 'Mad Bomber' because of his kamikaze approach. George rides an old 1-speed coaster brake machine with no front brake. His style is characterized by 75-foot sideways slides coming into corners, accompanied by miraculous recoveries. On one of his favourite roads, George crouches behind his handlebars and rides under a single pipe gate at 35-40 mph, and he claims jumps for distances of 40 feet.

Returning to the starting line we find that riders have been sent off at two-minute intervals. The spacing is to keep riders from catching and having to pass one another. The race evolved out of the downhill duelling that inevitably took place when groups of riders descended. A mass-start format was out of the question, because the narrow roads and blind corners inhibit passing, and any group larger than three was certain to invite mayhem. The time-trial format gives each rider the same chance, undistracted by other riders. By grouping the riders by ability the organisers prevent a slow rider from being followed by an extremely fast one.

The fastest riders are started last so the other finishers can observe their styles, and this starting order leads to an interesting psychological effect. As the number of riders at the line dwindles, those who remain are increasingly the most expert and dedicated riders. They all know each other, and while this is a friendly contest, it is still a contest and these riders are all trying to win it. After the first-time riders leave the line, the chatter dies down, and the air nearly turns blue with the fierce concentration now evident. The only sounds are soft noises of bike adjustments being made, broken now and then by the voice of the starter as he calls the next rider and counts down the start.

What is it like to ride this course? As the rider before you leaves, you have two minutes to prepare yourself, and for a surprising number this means a fast trip to the bushes for an emergency urination. Wheeling up to the line you find that your breathing is already a little strained, fast, and loud in your ears. 'Thirty seconds.' Squeeze brake levers for the hundredth time to make sure they are adjusted for maximum grab. 'Fifteen.' You check for the eighth time to make sure you are in the right gear. 'Ten.' Stand on the pedals as the starter holds your rear wheel. 'Five.' The world shrinks and becomes 12 feet wide, stretched out in front of you. It takes a conscious effort to hold back from an early start. 'GO!' The wheel is released and the bike shoots forward as if propelled by a tightly wound spring.

The first 150 yards are level with a soft surface and a light rise. It is imperative to ride this section as quickly as possible because the fast riders gain two or three seconds on the slower ones here.

Over the rise and into the downhill, and you are already gasping with the effort of the start. No time to let up though, because this section is straight and even though it is steep you are standing on your pedals and stomping your highest gear.

Blind left turn onto the steepest part of the course, covered with ruts and loose rocks. Watch the bump on the corner because at this speed it will launch you into the air and put you out of position for the next corner.

Now the road becomes a series of blind corners which all seem to look alike as you approach. This section favours the experienced Repack rider who can remember which corners to brake for and which can be taken wide open. Since Repack is in more or less a straight line at the top, most of these corners can be taken at full speed, a thrilling prospect in light of the fact that it will take you some distance to stop, unless you hit a tree. At no time should you stop pedalling unless you are jamming on the brakes. As you approach some of the more wicked curves you are conscious

**The Repack Test (failed)**

of a few 50-foot, side-to-side skid marks laid down by rookie riders. A definite 'groove' is visible on most corners, worn into the road surface by the passage of many knobby tyres.

A roller-coaster section gives you a new thrill as the bike becomes weightless just when you want the tyres on the ground. Into a dip and the bike slides, then corrects itself with no apparent help from the rider, and points in exactly the right direction. Cutting corners as closely as possible, you receive a whack or two from overhanging branches.

Your adrenalin pump goes into overdrive, and your reflexes and vision improve immeasurably. You are aware of every pebble on the road even though they are whipping past. You are completely alone; the only spectators are near the bottom. You dare not lose concentration for an instant, but there is little danger of that.

Sliding into an eroded, off-camber turn you make a slight miscalculation. Out of control, you must make a rapid decision, off the edge or lay the bike down. You lay it down . . .damn . . .torn shirt, bloody elbow. No time to check for further damage, since the arm still works; the shirt was old and the elbow was older. How's the bike? It's okay, and a little less paint won't affect the handling . . .jump back on and feed the chain back on as you coast the first few yards. Back in gear, and now you need to make up time.

Near the bottom of the course you reach the switchbacks, and now you are vaguely aware that you are being photographed as you try to maintain maximum speed through the hairpins. Out of the switchbacks in a cloud of dust and into the final straightaway. Jam on brakes to keep a bump from launching you off the edge. Now several dozen people line the edge of the roadway, earlier riders, girlfriends, and a few locals out to watch the action. Last corner . . .and speeding past the boulder that marks the finish, you skid to the flashiest possible stop, then throw down the bike and run over to the timer, who immediately gives you your elapsed time. It is the best recorded so far on the day, but your elation is reduced by the arrival of the next rider somewhat less than two minutes later. As the last half dozen riders finish, the times continue to go down, and the last finisher records the fastest time of the day, some twenty seconds better than yours. Any time under five minutes is respectable, but the record stands at 4:22.

Now the event is over and the winners are announced, but no prizes are handed out. There are no entry fees, very few rules, and usually no prizes other than a round of beers, but no-one seems to care. The finish line is a hubbub as adrenalised riders bounce around, reliving and describing at length their rides and various crashes. 'I would have done better, but I crashed . . . .' 'I crashed twice and still did better than you did . . . .' 'You should have seen it . . . .' But no-one did.

While the Repack race seems to define the essence of clunking, it is unique and is only one facet of the sport. Most clunker riders are interested primarily in riding, rather than racing. In northern California there is ample hill country, laced with fire roads and trails which are as good as motorways for clunker riders. This is where the clunker comes into its own, for these are not just downhill bikes. Super-low gears enable a strong rider to climb most hills, and the true enthusiast sees nothing wrong with spending an hour pushing his bike up a steep hill in order to come flying down. The clunker allows the rider to penetrate deep into the hills, away from cars and even from most hikers. The ability to travel at 10-15 mph in total silence in rough country makes the clunker the most efficient backwoods transportation yet invented. It can be ridden on the narrowest trails or carried if necessary over any obstacle.

As a means of transportation the clunker has a few drawbacks; weight (about 45 lb) and high rolling resistance due to the balloon tyres keeps the cruising speed down to a mellow but comfortable velocity. For short distances the clunker is a perfect vehicle, as its lack of speed is offset by incredible braking, cornering, and manoeuvreability. To the experienced rider there are no obstacles, and ditches, kerbs, fallen trees, and so on become part of the enjoyment of riding. One need not worry excessively about tyre damage since there is probably no more rugged bicycle tyre than the 2.125-inch knobbies in general clunker use.

Clunker technology, a field limited to a small number of mad cyclo-scientists, is still in its infancy. Plans are being developed for frames to be made of the same lightweight tubing used in racing bicycles. If the weight can be brought down and the frame redesigned for better handling the machines in use will become as obsolete as the bikes they were made from. In under-developed countries, such as America, the clunker has promise as low-cost, non-polluting transportation over any terrain.

# Repack Revisited

The Repack Downhill is gone, the victim of its own success. Originally an underground event, with the increasing numbers of mountain bikers it surfaced on a nationally syndicated television programme in 1979. Instead of a couple of dozen friends the field grew to upwards of 100 riders, and this attracted the attention of the government agencies who owned the property the road runs across. Attempts to work within the system by acquiring all necessary permits failed in the harsh light of the liability and insurance situation. The last Repack race was run in 1984.

In some respects, despite the fact that it was the point of origin for much of the mountain bike movement, the Repack event cast mountain biking in a bad light. Because it was a spectacular event, it drew attention from the main focus of mountain biking, simply riding on rough roads. And because it also exemplified the riding style that has come to be described as 'gonzo', i.e., all-out with no regard for personal safety (and by implication for the safety of others), those elements of society who consider bicycles a dangerous intrusion in wilderness areas have seized upon this race as an embodiment of everyone's worst fears.

In its history from 1976 to 1984, Repack saw no more than 200 individuals take part. In spite of this, the name has assumed legendary status among mountain bikers. This status may or may not be deserved, but it is certain that this unlikely event was the meeting place and testing site for the people who brought mountain biking to the world. Among the participants were course record-holder Gary Fisher, who helped put gears on Marin's 'clunkers', and who is also responsible for some of the standard refinements by adding 'thumb-shifters' and the quick-release seat clamp. Joe Breeze holds the second-fastest time, and his designs and frame building were the breakthrough that created the modern mountain bike. Tom Ritchey raced at Repack on a borrowed Schwinn Excelsior before he ever built a mountain bike; Tom's influence can still be seen in the designs of most mass-produced mountain bikes. Another early builder, Erik Koski, raced his designs there. For my part, I was the race organiser, scorer, and Keeper of the Records; in 1976 I had a frame built specifically for the purpose of racing there, the first custom mountain bike I know of. (This frame did not live up to my expectations, so I persuaded Joe Breeze to build me another one. Two—his and mine—turned into ten, the prototypes of the modern machine.)

As it turned out, the northern California riders were not the only people experimenting with off-road bicycles. A noted cycling enthusiast named John Finley Scott had built in 1953 a bike which in nearly all respects resembled the generation of off-road bikes that followed the first modified news-boy bikes of the sort first raced at Repack. Scott's bike had a Schwinn World diamond frame, knobby tyres, derailleur gears, and upright handlebars. Just before the beginning of the mountain bike revolution, during the early 1970s, ranchers in Arizona were using knobby-tyre bikes with 5-speed gearing to inspect their vast acreages.

But these examples and no doubt others like them seemed to be isolated, and they failed to influence the rest of the cycling world. By 1979 several Northern California builders were making major strides in off-road design, inspired by the feedback from each other's efforts. In addition to Joe Breeze, these included Erik Koski, Jeffrey Richman, Jeff Lindsay, and of course Tom Ritchey.

In 1979 Ritchey's frames became the first offered on the market commercially. Even at the staggering price of about $1,300 a copy, he could not keep up with the orders. About the same time Marin County brothers Don and Erik Koski designed the 'Trailmaster', and shortly afterward Jeff Lindsay introduced his 'Mountain Goat'. In 1980 Specialized Bicycle Imports of San Jose, California, bought four of Ritchey's bikes and used them as the starting point for the design of the first mass-produced mountain bike, the Japanese-made Stumpjumper, which appeared in 1981. With the appearance of this and other mass-market bikes shortly afterward, the movement took off.

# CHAPTER 2

# The Original Clunkers

In the beginning of the off-road movement, getting a suitable clunker was not a question of zipping down to the bike shop and forking out the necessary ducats. Getting a bike was more akin to a scavenger hunt, in which participants had to go to a number of unlikely locations and pick up seemingly unrelated items, before attempting to fit together a pile of non-standard parts. Because of the hassle it took to put one together, those who had the expertise in assembly could charge up to $400 for a clunker built on a forty-year-old frame, at a time when that amount would buy a fairly fancy road bike. Often people unfamiliar with Marin clunkers would see one of these bikes and, noting the practicality, would ask casually how much one like it would cost. The answer would send them reeling. 'Four hundred? For this rusty thing?'

Of course, prices for mass-produced bikes are based on the economy of scale. By building thousands of identical bikes and by getting the components directly from the factories, manufacturers can keep the cost within reason. Clunker builders had to spend considerable time and money (usually at retail rather than manufacturer's prices) before beginning the assembly process, which did not take place on an efficient assembly line but in a garage or back yard. After building a few bikes at cost for friends, those who had acquired the necessary skills, tools, parts, and experience to make the standard Marin County conversion realised that it was a waste of time unless the profit motive was invoked.

The first order of business in getting together a clunker was obtaining a frame. By 1976 the supply of unbroken balloon-tyre frames in Marin County had been mined heavily, and scroungers were making trips far afield looking for new supplies. On a trip to a part of California about 200 miles from the Bay Area I found a farmer who had a pile of rusting bikes behind his house. I bought about five excellent frames, and more importantly acquired a pile of unbent forks. After I gloated about my good fortune at home, several of my friends went back and cleaned the farmer out of everything else of any use, including a couple of frames I hadn't noticed.

One of the facts of life among clunker riders was bent forks. To begin with, nearly any bike forty years old had already been through a few dozen head-on collisions, and the cheesy, flat-bladed non-tubular forks almost never survived as well as the rest of the frame. Even if they did, the new owner would generally finish them off in short order, and the average clunker rider expected to use up a couple of pairs of forks a year. Old girls' bike frames were unsuitable for riding, but for some reason girls didn't use up nearly as many forks as the owners of boys' frames, so old girls' frames were discarded after being stripped of everything useful, primarily the fork and coaster brake hub.

The 'knee-action' sprung fork that appeared on some of the fancier Schwinns in the forties and fifties was the subject of a never-to-be-repeated experiment. For one thing, the fork was too heavy even for a clunker rider who wasn't adverse to hanging all kinds of other heavy objects from his frame. Also, while the knee action might smooth out some of the ruts while the bike travelled in a straight line, it gave the bike a continuously changing wheelbase and head angle through a corner and absorbed the rider's energy whenever he stood up to pedal. This component inspired the phrase: 'It doesn't work, but at least it's ugly'.

Although their value in preserving the integrity of the fork may be questioned, every Marin clunker rider who could find them sported on his bike a pair of 'fork braces', steel rods running from the headset to the drop-out. Whatever their value, they gave the Marin bikes another of their distinctive features.

In my travels during that period I was careful to look for the oldest bike shop in every town I visited, and I made a point to ask there if they had any old stuff lying around that I could poke through. Most of the time it was nothing but junk, but the times I struck gold were worth any number of disappointments. I can remember finding a fruit crate full of Morrow coaster brakes in a small town in Northern California, buying rare Schwinn cantilever brakes for a couple of dollars in Stockton, and the time in Denver I stumbled on literally dozens of Bendix coaster brake 2-speed hubs, complete with shifters and cables. Keep in mind that these parts were as good as money in the small sphere of clunker riders.

After obtaining the parts, the prospective clunker builder did not just sit down and throw them together over a period of a few hours. Usually the process took from several days to a week, and included half a dozen trips to the bike shop and a couple to the hardware store. No matter how many lists were made out, it always seemed to take one more trip for parts.

Step one of the building process was realigning the frame. The rear drop-out width was not wide enough for the derailleur gearing set up, and required careful spreading. The trick was keeping everything aligned so the rear wheel would still be in the middle. This was accomplished by careful prying with a two-by-four and a little subtle stomping, with a piece of string tied around the frame to check for straightness. The process was accompanied by incantations of the four-letter variety. The frame alignment was rarely permanent, since the frames were made of small diameter mild steel rather than the oversize chrome-moly used now, and realignment was necessary now and then for bikes that saw heavy service, until the frame gave up the ghost at one of the overstressed welds.

Two-speed coaster brake hubs were the first step toward multiple gearing on clunkers. The Bendix company made two varieties of this component, one that was shifted by a lever and cable, and one that was shifted by back-pedalling. The cable-operated type was much preferred, since on the other type each application of the brakes shifted the gear.

One gearing experiment involved the use of an internally shifting 3-speed hub used in conjunction with a 3-speed cluster and derailleur for a 9-speed combination. Three-speed hubs with drum brakes were available, and this looked like a promising direction. The compound low gear of about 18 inches was attractive; with a pair of 185 mm cranks the rider should be able to ride straight up a wall. That was the theory. In practice the internal gearing was not capable of handling the torque developed by a bike-and-rider combination weighing over 250 pounds, using these long cranks, and attempting to climb a tree. The internal planetary gears exploded into dust on the first steep climb and the experiment was declared a failure.

Although Gary Fisher is generally credited with being the first person to try a drum brake 5-speed hub on his clunker, he should be more properly credited with being the first person from Marin County to do so. In 1974 the California state cyclo-cross championships were held in Marin, a low-key affair, since the 'Bike Boom' was just getting under way. Two of the participants, who did not live in the area, rode balloon-tyre bikes equipped with multiple gearing and drum rear brakes. To this day I have no idea who these men were, but had they continued to work in that vein, one of them might have been writing this book!

Nearly a year later, Gary Fisher found an old tandem rear drum brake at a flea market and brought it home. Any of us who hefted it thought that the massive steel hub was too heavy to be of any use, but Gary went ahead and built a wheel on it. The process involved a typical clunker adaptation, since Gary was unable to find the correct length of spokes. He shortened some by bending them an inch or so from the spoke head and hooking them through the flange.

The drum hub added more weight to an already heavy bike, but Gary convinced all his sceptical friends on the first ride with his 5-speed bike. In spite of the extra weight, he pulled away on a long hill so convincingly that within a week drum rear brakes had been added to the list of items to be obtained whenever they were available.

Marin County has more than its share of bike shops, and suddenly all of them were besieged by clunker riders demanding tandem drum brakes. This was the sort of item that the average shop might sell once in ten years, and suddenly it was the hottest component around. The sudden demand for the obscure part was likely the first indication to the bike industry that something unusual was going on there. After the second or third reorder, Marin bike shops dragged their drum brake hubs out of the

**Gary Fisher on the Repack where he set the course record. Inset: As the modern-day mountain bike manufacturer**

**Gary Fisher's original 5-speed drum brake clunker, c.1974**

back room and began displaying them as prominently as such a fast-moving item deserved. No doubt the wholesalers who supplied the shops began to notice that most of the drum brakes sold in the United States were going to one obscure location.

Front drum brakes were popular also; the only practical alternative was a rare pair of Schwinn cantilever brakes that bolted directly to the fork blades. The most stylish front drum brake to have was the original equipment Arnold-Schwinn drum brake, but this was as rare as the cantilevers. Riders scrounged for a variety of drums made in Scandinavia and England. Another source was a front drum brake drilled for 24 spokes and used as original equipment on a line of Schwinn 20-inch bikes. Riders re-drilled them for 36 holes.

Having converted their bikes to multiple gears, clunker riders now needed a proper shifting assembly. Down tube shifters didn't work, because for one thing the diameter of the down tube on an old clunker was too small for the clamp, and for another, riders decided that they didn't want to be reaching for the shifter while going over rough ground. The obvious solution is bar-end shifters, but these met with limited favour because they could easily snag on brush on a narrow trail and could be snapped off in a crash. At first riders tried 'stem shifters', which are found on cheap 10-speeds and mount on the stem right over the headset. The problem with these was that the rider still had to take his hands off the bars to shift, and when he stood up, he could hit them with his knees.

One early solution was to mount the stem shifters on the handlebar near the right grip. This permitted the rider to shift with his hands on the bars, and considering the alternatives it was no trouble to handle all the shifting with one hand. Gary Fisher deserves credit for adapting the 'thumb-shifter' to clunker use. If off-road bikes had not come along, this component might have drifted into the obscurity it was headed for, since until that time thumb-shifters were only found on inexpensive ladies' middleweights. For some years in fact, thumb-shifters were made only for the right side, since the original design was for the rear derailleur only. Clunker riders became used to the asymmetrical shifters, using a right for a left by turning the clamp around.

Gary Fisher's other major contribution to clunker design was the introduction of the quick-release seat post clamp. Modern mountain bikes use a cam-type quick-release similar to an axle quick-release, but the QRs used on early clunkers were more commonly threaded screw-down seat post tighteners taken from stationary exercisers. The reason for using this device is so the saddle could be lowered during descents, but clunker riders had reasons for lowering the saddle that weren't related to the centre of gravity. The old frames used a small diameter seat post made of mild steel, which was nowhere near as strong as the larger diameter alloy seat posts used on racing bikes. Clunker frames were of the 'one size fits all' variety, and for the 6-foot-plus riders this meant that in order to get proper leg extension they had to expose a considerable length of seat post. If the rider landed heavily on the saddle during a bouncing, rocky downhill, it usually bent the seat post. Saddles were lowered to prevent this possibility by reducing the amount of leverage that could be applied to the seat post.

Speaking of seat posts brings up the subject of saddles. The saddle of choice during the early clunker movement was the Brooks B-72, a wide leather platform supported on four rails rather than the more common two-rail arrangement. Modern mountain bikes have saddles similar to those found on road bikes, but the early clunker riders wanted something wider. The only problems with the B-72 were, one, durability and two, finding one. Problem one was solved by having a few extras in the parts box, but problem two took careful scrounging. Of course, anyone who wanted to go into a shop and spend $30 could have a B-72, but this was not the spirit of the times. The trick was to find an old Raleigh 3-speed, which featured the B-72 as original equipment; after terminal neglect had set in and the only useful part left was the saddle, the entire bike could be purchased for a couple of dollars.

One of the features that sets mountain bikes apart from standard road bikes is the upright handlebar. Clunker riders didn't have the modern versions of one-piece 'bullmoose' type or the other refined handlebars that have been developed by custom mountain bike builders. Instead they used a variety of unusual handlebars; one style popular with the early 1-speed clunkers was the 'longhorn' swept-back bars that were original equipment on the old frames. As the multiple-geared clunkers became popular, riders opted for handlebars designed for BMX or motorcycles. At first the style was to get the biggest and widest available, but the problems these caused on narrow trails influenced riders to cut them down to a more reasonable size.

Along with the thumb-shifters, riders mounted motorcycle brake levers on their handlebars. These were used because the only bicycle brake levers made for flat handlebars were cheap specimens that were not up to the rugged treatment they received off-road. The motorcycle levers had threaded cable adjusters which proved useful in a time when drum brakes required constant attention and adjustment. In addition, the longer motorcycle lever provided more leverage.

With the introduction of the 5-speed clunker by Gary Fisher, the 10-speed was the obvious next step. Even if they didn't plan to use ten gears, riders found that they had to mount a front derailleur as a chain guide, since the chain would derail off the front ring when the bike started bouncing down a steep hill. Once the derailleur was in place, it seemed silly not to find an old Schwinn Varsity steel double chainwheel on a one-piece crank and mount it up.

Alloy cranksets had to wait until the special adapter necessary to mount cotterless cranks to the 2-inch bottom bracket shell was available. Just as they had done with handlebars, riders turned to parts created by the rapid rise in popularity of BMX. Even though the 20-inch bikes were considerably smaller than clunker bikes, they used the same standards for parts such as headsets and bottom brackets. At this time BMX riders were demanding higher quality cranksets, which led manufacturers to introduce the necessary adapters. This permitted clunker riders to upgrade to alloy cranksets with considerably more variety in gearing than the steel one-piece.

# Meanwhile in the Rockies

## *1978*

Crested Butte, Colorado, a small town located high in the Rocky Mountains, is the scene of what is certainly one of the most unusual bicycle tours in this country. Not to be confused with traditional bicycle touring, in which a 10-speed bike is loaded with camping gear and directed down a smooth ribbon of asphalt, the 'Crested Butte to Aspen Klunker Tour' pits a ragtag collection of balloon-tyre bicycles and free spirits against some of the roughest terrain ever attempted on two wheels. The result is a two-day expression of exuberance reminiscent of frontier festivities.

Crested Butte, sometimes called Crusty Butt by the locals, is an isolated town with a population of about 1,500. The elevation of nearly 9,000 feet is rendered insignificant by the surrounding mountains, massive, treeless peaks ranging from 12,000 to over 14,000 feet. The town boasts just two surfaced streets, and except for the presence of motor vehicles, it still looks like a mining town straight out of the 1880s. Half the buildings do not appear to have been painted since they were built in the last century. In its longest dimension, Crested Butte measures no more than ten blocks.

Distances and road conditions being what they are, there is little need in Crested Butte for a $1,000, 19-pound, handcrafted Italian racing bicycle. It is no more than a five-minute ride for the slowest cyclist on the heaviest bike from any part of town to any other, and in the last few years most of the citizens under the age of forty have equipped themselves with some form of 'town bike', assembled from whatever parts are available. While the local bike shop (operated out of the proprietor's living-room) has access to a few new parts, the main supply of components comes from occasional expeditions to a rich vein, the Denver Dump.

The people of Crested Butte are an individualistic collection, since the long winters and limited local economy combine to keep out all but the hardiest souls. During the short summer many of the men work on the forest fire crews, putting in long days of hard work under dangerous conditions for $4.50 an hour. The cultural gulf between Crested Butte and Aspen, 35 air miles but over 100 driving miles away, is enormous. Aspen is well known as the home of celebrities in the fields of sports, motion pictures, and recording. In Aspen people Have Money; in Crested Butte people Make a Living.

Given the cultural differences, it isn't surprising that the good ol' boys from Crested Butte consider their counterparts in Aspen somewhat effete. As long as the Aspen residents stayed on their side of the mountain they could be ignored, but in the summer of 1976 a group of motorcyclists from Aspen rode over rugged 12,700-foot Pearl Pass; when they reached Crested Butte they parked their machines in a row in front of the Grubstake Saloon and stepped inside to wash down the dust.

The Grubstake was the main watering hole for the Crested Butte fire-fighting crowd, although they didn't drink much water there, and they weren't impressed by what they viewed as a cultural intrusion. Ringleader Rick Verplank sensed a need to top the invasion from Aspen with a gesture from Crested Butte, and came up with the idea of duplicating the feat on town bikes and parking a pile of typical Crested Butte machinery in front of the biggest bar in Aspen.

The first epic ride was carried off in fine style, even though some 'riders' covered much of the distance by travelling in one of the several 4-wheel-drive vehicles that accompanied the group. The group took two days to reach Aspen, camping out for the night at Cumberland Basin at 11,000 feet. Richard ('Richard the Rat') Ullery achieved some notoriety on the trip; hampered by a broken leg but not to be left out, he followed the cyclists in a support vehicle riding in a padded, antique copper bathtub. The event was such a success that plans were laid to make the ride an annual event sponsored by the Grubstake Saloon.

The next year, 1977, was a dry year, and most of the original riders were too occupied with fire-fighting duties to take part. The Second Annual Klunker Tour was cancelled. The dry summer was followed by a dry winter, and the local skiers were frustrated by an absence of snow. As an outlet for the accumulated energy they staged impromptu town bike events, such as a lap race on a course in the middle of town that started on the main street and threaded its way through back yards and a frozen 6-foot-wide alley. Another event called for blocking the street in front of the Grubstake for a bike-jumping distance contest off a 2-foot ramp; this led to an enormously satisfying amount of personal and mechanical destruction.

During this same period on the West Coast, a number of northern California cyclists including myself had been experimenting with cross-country bicycles. For the most part these were old balloon-tyre frames converted to multiple-gear derailleur systems, using drum brakes but retaining the balloon tyres. In 1977 these bikes had been taken a step farther with the construction of a few handmade prototypes. The frames for these new bikes are made for 26-inch balloon-tyre wheels and the geometry is copied from a popular bike from the thirties, but there any resemblance to the old 'news-boy' bike ends. All the tubing is straight chrome-moly instead of curved mild steel, and all components are high-quality bicycle parts such as sealed-bearing hubs and bottom bracket, and brazed-on cantilever brakes. Twelve gears with the emphasis on the low range make these the ultimate mountain bikes.*

When the Crested Butte to Aspen ride came to our attention through a magazine article we contacted Duane Reading and Bob Starr, owners of the Grubstake Saloon, and they informed us that the ride was on again and was scheduled for September 23 and 24 with the same camp-out at Cumberland Basin. A 4-wheel-drive vehicle would carry all the gear, so cyclists were free to enjoy themselves while pushing their bikes 8 or 10 miles uphill. The ride sounded like an interesting challenge and a great time, so with as little planning as possible, five of us from California made our way to Crested Butte, where we joined some of the local citizens in what turned out to be a unique experience.

Entering Crested Butte on a beautiful afternoon, our first impression was that everyone in town owned a bike. Most of the machines were the products of years of cross-breeding: a 10-speed, for example, might be modified by the addition of fatter tyres, a banana seat, and high-rise handlebars (with ribbons on the ends) so that a person may sit properly upright and observe his or her surroundings. Since the streets are so rough and the distances short, the old balloon-tyre bikes with 1-speed and kick-back coaster brakes are more popular than skinny-tyre 10-speeds. The average speed of a cyclist in Crested Butte is usually just enough to keep the machine upright; the stately and graceful progress of the citizens harkens back to a gentler era and is itself an argument against the use of the automobile.

On our arrival we searched out Duane Reading at the Grubstake and introduced ourselves, and in turn he introduced us to just about everyone in Crested Butte. The arrival of a truck loaded with strange bicycles did not go unnoticed, and within a short time most of the locals who would eventually accompany us to Aspen had checked us out and inspected our bikes.

After introductions and shop talk with the town bike mechanics we were hustled over to the local radio station for a live interview, since we were the closest thing to news that had happened all week. The disc jockey was taken by surprise, so we all sat in the tiny studio and tried to think of clever things to say. Failing in this, we were saved by the bell, figuratively speaking, in the form of the town fire alarm, which assured us that no-one was listening.

As might be expected the Crested Butte boys are maniacal downhill riders, having hundreds of miles of steep dirt roads close at hand. On a slow afternoon some of the crew get a truck ride to the top of a convenient local peak and then ride back to town in a wild rush on the challenging terrain. After our 'interview' Duane suggested that we go out to a favourite local downhill, a long, steep hill with the reassuring

---

* This was written in 1978 and was probably the first time the term 'mountain bike' appeared in print.

**Media hype Crested Butte-style**

name, 'The Ride to Die'. After a couple of days of driving, we were ready for some action, so we jumped at the offer.

The first order of business was rounding up a truck to take us out there, and Duane took care of that by stopping every pick-up coming down the street, looking for a volunteer driver. The process took a little while, but eventually we climbed into a wheezing old Chevy truck piloted by a madman and headed out of town. The trip up one side of the ridge was at least as exciting as the trip down the other side on bikes, as our driver kept his dying vehicle in motion by hoarding his momentum, holding the pedal to the floor on the level stretches and hitting the steep pitches as fast as possible. On the last turn before the summit the truck balked, so we all piled out while the driver backed off 100 yards for a flying attempt. Amid a cloud of dust, blue smoke, and profanity, the truck made what was certainly its last assault on the ridge, since by this time the cab was alarmingly full of smoke.

The scenery on top of the ridge was, as expected, spectacular, so we spent a few minutes taking it all in before starting down toward Crested Butte. The Ride to Die is a typical Rocky Mountain back road, steep, rocky, eroded, rough, and lots of fun. The first half-mile or so resembled a streambed, pure loose rock and gravel, then it changed to a smooth dirt surface with a few surprises such as scattered large rocks or deep erosion ditches which here and there cut completely across the road. The best way to handle the ditches is to approach at high speed and lift the front wheel at exactly the right time; the consequences of poor timing are obvious, but we all had plenty of experience at this and there were no mishaps. Near the bottom we encountered several sweeping curves, and as we entered these all the members of our group were whooping and screaming with exhilaration. The combination of the fine weather, beautiful surroundings and great riding overwhelmed our senses and created one of those jewels of experience that stands in the memory as a time when everything was perfect.

Reaching the bottom of the ridge we found a gently sloping valley floor which was shared equally between beavers and cattle. We were immediately impressed by the ingenuity of the beavers, expressed in their elaborate water projects, contrasted with the stupidity of the cattle. Perhaps thinking we were cowboys there to round them up, a couple of dozen cattle trotted down the road in front of us in a slow-motion stampede until Joe cut across the rough field to outflank them and herd them off the road while we passed. None of the beavers stampeded.

On the rolling road our group stretched out as each of us found his own pace. We regrouped at the Grubstake after riding the three or four miles of smooth dirt road back to town, and Duane offered us the use of his house during our stay. Having put no previous thought to the matter of a place to sleep, we accepted rapidly.

The next morning dawned warm and clear, and with one day to kill before the big ride, we set out to explore Crested Butte. Our first stop was the local living-room bike shop, where the proprietors were busy getting their own machines ready. The shop is in an old house with a yard full of wheels, frames, and bikes either partially assembled or disassembled depending on one's point of view.

From the shop we wandered over to a house on the other side of town where the unfenced front lawn was strewn with bike parts, tyres, wheels, cans of solvent, spray paint, and assorted nameless fragments. Here a group that varied from three to nine people conducted all day what can only be described as creative bike repairs. There had been talk of cancelling the ride due to extreme lack of local participation, but our arrival had changed all that. After all, we even had a woman in our group, and no Crested Butte fire-fighter was about to admit that she was capable of something he wasn't. Unfortunately, until we arrived no-one had given much thought to bicycle maintenance, and at this late date the situation was universally desperate among the locals. With the only real bike mechanics in town hard at work on their own bikes there was a shortage of labour, so we pitched in to help out some of the worst cases.

Due to the lack of new parts, some bikes were ruthlessly pirated in order that others might live. Minor differences in components make a ball-peen hammer an essential tool in this operation. These eleventh hour efforts left little time for testing of the results; the test would come the next day, and some would fail it.

Later that evening most of the fire-fighters gathered at the Grubstake for what appeared to be some kind of purification ritual. They toasted each other until they were all completely toasted.

As we assembled casually the next morning in front of the Grubstake there were obvious differences between the California crew and the local riders. On our side were the dedicated cyclists on the custom machinery, in addition to myself, Joe Breeze, Gary Fisher, Mike Castelli, and Wende Cragg. By contrast the locals were not so involved with cycling as they were involved in doing outrageous things, such as dragging town bikes over the pass. They were surprised that anyone would travel 1,000 miles to do anything so ridiculous. Eight riders from Crested Butte took part, along with one from Denver and another from Hotchkiss, about 50 miles away. A local retriever named Chump, owned by local 'Archie' Archuleta, lent mascot support.

We piled camping gear into two 4-wheel-drive vehicles that would act as motorized support. In the lead would be Tour organiser Duane Reading, and following us would be jeep acting as sagwagon and carrying a photographer. For an hour or so moderate confusion reigned as riders compared bikes, took pictures, and packed the support vehicles. A small crowd of spectators had gathered, since this was the only visible activity in town, so no-one was in a hurry to leave and give up all this attention.

At eleven o'clock we finally assembled for an 'official' start. The point was repeatedly and loudly made that this was a tour and not a race, as we lined up sixteen strong (some stronger than others) from kerb to kerb. Duane impatiently directed the limited auto traffic onto other streets, and surprised drivers muttered imprecations as they were told in no uncertain terms that this street was in use and they would have to use another. A few more photos were taken, and then Duane shouted 'Go!' We were off on the great adventure.

Repeated assertions notwithstanding, the start of the ride resembled a race as the group tore down Elk Avenue, still using the entire width of the street along with the pavement and a few front lawns. At the edge of town we joined the highway for about two miles, and the group strung out immediately as the experienced riders dropped into a pace line. The pace slackened as soon as we turned off onto the dirt road, and we regrouped, riding slowly together for a few miles and marvelling at the fine weather and perfect conditions.

The first real climb was short, but it opened a gap, so as we rolled onto level ground the leaders called for a rest stop, no more than four miles into the ride. As the slower riders rolled up, the reason for the gap became obvious; some of the riders were showing the effects of heavy bar training in the form of nearly terminal hangovers.

While we rested, Albert discovered that his bike had been sabotaged with grease on the rear rim, rendering his calliper brake useless. No one claimed credit, but all were amused as it was cleaned off. Bob Starr, who was hung far over, demonstrated his version of a purification ritual by returning his breakfast. This was greeted by a round of the 'Golf Clap', a politely restrained, almost inaudible form of applause which in Crested Butte is reserved for dubious achievements.

We shoved off again, and were stopped immediately by a flat tyre on Archie's bike. If it was possible, Archie was in even worse shape than Bob Starr, and he looked as though he might cry as he surveyed his tyre and considered his alternatives. Joe Breeze took over. He was well equipped with tools and a spare tube, and in a few minutes he had removed the wheel and replaced the tube. The account of this incident in the *Crested Butte Chronicle* reflected the local awe of the California skills. It read as follows: 'The California boys immediately jack-knifed into action; tools selected after years of experience glimmered in the sunlight as the intrepid Californians removed the wheel, replaced the tube, tuned the spokes, remounted the wheel, slacked the cones a tad, adjusted the chain, and had Archie's bike back on the road in 35 seconds flat!'

The cause of the flat tyre was found to be part of a 3-speed shifting mechanism that had somehow found its way inside the casing. This revelation was greeted by another round of the Golf Clap as we got under way.

The quality of the road surface continued to deteriorate as the scenery improved. Climbing and dropping along the side of a lush valley we made several shallow creek crossings, giving us an opportunity to test and/or demonstrate the various methods for riding through water. By the time we reached the deepest crossing, which was over the hubs, the group had strung out again, so the lead riders called a halt on the far side. The stop was not so much for rest or regrouping as it was to watch everyone else try to ford the creek.

The follow-up vehicle arrived with the last riders, so in the absence of any real leadership the group decided it was time for lunch and a few beers. By this time Cloud's springer fork had fallen apart and the bolt holding his high-rise handlebars had broken, so more repairs were necessary. Nearly an hour passed before another spontaneous group decision was made to push on.

By this time it was well into the afternoon, and everyone proceeded at his or her own pace with no further efforts to regroup. Archie immediately took a nap. The terrain from here to the camp site was rugged and climbed sharply, so with the advantage of having lower gears, our California group was first into camp at Cumberland Basin, 11,000 feet elevation. Duane had already arrived with all the essentials, food, sleeping bags, and a keg of beer, which was shaken up by the rough ride. Riders straggled into camp for the next hour and a half, and bikes and bodies were thrown on the ground as everyone tried to find a lungful of what passed for air at this elevation.

By this time a clear sky had given way to clouds, and a few anxious eyes were turned skyward. Those with tents pitched them immediately and some of those without regaled the rest with the information that on the first epic Pearl Pass ride it had rained heavily during the night. A few drops of rain fell, then the threat moved on and by sunset the sky was clear. In contrast to near record cold several nights previously, the temperature stayed around 50°F all night, rare and wonderful conditions for this altitude and time of year.

Dinner was steaks cooked on a camp fire 3 feet across and potatoes baked in the coals. After dinner the camp fire was stoked with a couple of foot-thick logs, and, as we relaxed around it, we were treated to tales of amazing exploits by the locals and graphic descriptions of the first Pearl Pass ride. There was some discussion of the proper methods and the problems of cooking lunch while fighting a forest fire. 'You look around for a nice hot spot, and as soon as you find it and go to get your food, some jerk comes over and puts it out!' Some of the stories were entering into their third renditions by the time we slipped off to bed.

The next morning dawned warm but overcast. The fire was stirred back to life and one by one the group crawled out of scattered sleeping bags and assembled around it. Breakfast was cantaloup and OJ, but Duane, who didn't drink coffee, hadn't brought any, and he was subjected to a stream of abuse for the sin of omission. With one day's removal from their watering hole, the fire-fighters were a little more clear of

**Line-up for the Crested Butte Annual Klunker Tour, 1979**

eye. No-one seemed to be in much of a hurry to break camp, but eventually all the gear was loaded onto the truck, which headed back toward Crested Butte. Leaving with the truck were local rider Susan and the retriever Chump. The Denver rider announced his retirement also, and headed back to town as the rest of us started the final assault. From here our only motorized support was the jeep, and it was barely capable of making some of the steeper pitches.

After much procrastination a gradual exodus began from the camp. Starr was offering encouraging gems of coaching wisdom such as, '. . . when the going gets tough, the stupid get going'. The going got tough. We covered the 3½ miles to the summit at a plodding pace, and our bikes had to be pushed, dragged, and carried over most of the distance. Above treeline there was little dirt, and the road surface became slabs of loose rock. Gasping, aching, and stumbling over rocks, we were in a bike rider's version of heaven.

The climb to the barren summit of the pass at 12,700 feet elevation took most of the crew nearly two hours. Having recovered from their hangovers, the fire-fighters were tougher than we had given them credit for being. Based on his performance from the previous day we had thought the climb would finish off Bob Starr, but like the train that thought it could, he trudged up the road on nothing but mental strength, his body having given out the day before.

Having expended so much energy to get to the top, no-one was in a hurry to leave,

so snacks were passed around, tyre pressures were checked, pictures taken, and the excellent echo demonstrated by a burst of alpine yodelling.

As we rested, who should arrive from the Aspen side of the pass, but a half-dozen motorcyclists. These were the kind of people we were here to impress, and their arrival couldn't have been more perfectly timed. They gave us great satisfaction by assuring us that we were as crazy as we had hoped we were.

The road over the pass was built in 1882 for mule trains to take ore from Aspen to the railhead at Crested Butte. Looking at it was enough to impress us with the hardiness of Colorado mules. It strains the imagination to picture even a powerful team dragging a wagon load of rocks up here. There has been no maintenance of the road since the twenties, and much of what we were about to ride down resembled a streambed more than it did a road.

The wind was biting, so when no more excuses were available everyone lined up across the top of the descent. While the last few pictures were taken we reminded each other that this was a tour and not a race, '. . . but don't get in my way while I'm touring!' Finally Starr boomed out, 'As elder statesman of the Crested Butte to Aspen Bike ride, I declare the course . . . OPEN!' Fourteen riders tried to elbow their ways into the lead of the 'tour', but the rough and narrow road soon stretched out the group.

It took half an hour to cover the 7 miles downhill to the paved road, and during that time the sensation was similar to that of being strapped to a paint shaker. Arms and legs were soon aching from absorbing shock and hands went numb and blistered from hanging on to the brake levers. There was relief in stopping, but doing so would allow other riders to pass, something no-one was willing to allow. Even so, no-one covered the 7 miles without stopping to rest. Richard the Rat was put out of action when his coaster brake shattered; he continued for a short way by jamming his foot against the front tyre and by plunging into convenient snowbanks, but he was forced to pack it in and ride into Aspen in the sagwagon.

When we reached the paved road the going became easy, 15 miles downhill with a tail wind on smooth paved roads. We stopped just outside the Aspen city limit, where Starr issued each of us balloons. We put these on the bikes so they would rub on the spokes and make the schoolyard motorcycle sound. Then we rode into Aspen and vroomed to the chosen public house to park our bikes in a row and brag. Our support drivers had purchased a case of beer, which we set on the pavement while we celebrated and carried on. When we told curious passers-by what we were up to, they would walk away shaking their heads.

We had all paid $15 for the privilege of going on the ride, and Starr had with him all that was left after our expenditures for food, beer, and gas. Taking this into the saloon, he laid it on the bar and the serious bragging began. Starr, who had been saying, 'Never again', was already talking about next year's ride and what a great support driver he would make because now he knew the road so well.

There was some disorganisation concerning transportation back to Crested Butte, and as the afternoon wore on and no-one showed up to get us, the pessimists started thinking about what it would be like to ride back over Pearl Pass. Finally a beat-up flat-bed truck with no silencer and a flat tyre roared into town to pick us up. After repairing the tyre, we piled all the bikes and most of our persons into the back and made ourselves as comfortable as possible for the three-hour drive back.

## Crested Butte Revisited

Since the preceding account was written, a lot of dirt has passed under a lot of tyres. The hand-made prototypes we rode in Crested Butte were further refined, and in turn gave birth to the mass-produced mountain bike, or All-Terrain Bicycle.

In the decade that has passed, Crested Butte has itself changed. Now most of the streets are properly surfaced, and the town has grown. The Annual Klunker Tour has changed considerably, and is now a major event on the town's autumn calendar. Symptomatic of the changes is the fact that none of the original fire-fighters goes on the ride any more; a new generation of cyclists rides the finest handmade custom mountain bikes instead of patched-together 'town bikes'. In fact, the ratio of expensive mountain bikes per capita in the town must be the highest in the United States. The town has gone crazy for mountain bikes, and each autumn the third week in September is dubbed 'Fat Tire Bike Week', a cycling celebration capped by the Pearl Pass Tour.

The Tour has outgrown itself in some respects. With upwards of 300 riders showing up for the event, the support logistics became impossible, especially since the Pearl Pass road is now virtually impassable in places to any form of 4-wheel ransportation. Rather than focusing on the tour, Fat Tire Bike Week has become a series of one-day rides in the mountains, along with races, picnics, and other activities for cyclists. Because of its reputation as the home of several top riders and the many roads and trails available, Crested Butte has served as the de facto training camp for mountain bike racers training for the national championships. Other areas have used Fat Tire Bike Week as the model for similar events, and now the recreational mountain biker has several 'Bike Weeks' to choose from.

Aside from all the other activities that take place during Fat Tire Bike Week, the Pearl Pass Tour itself has attained a status comparable to a pilgrimage. Since Bike Week organisers have withdrawn motorized support, riders trek without benefit of sag support to the top of Pearl Pass. Some continue over into Aspen, but most spend a few moments at this beautiful but otherwise undistinguished and remote location before the chill wind drives them back down the valley to Crested Butte. The ride takes an energetic rider all day, and the last 3 miles to the top can take a couple of hours.

Once the mecca for all serious mountain bikers, Fat Tire Bike Week has seen its importance diluted by the host of other mountain bike events springing up all over the country. Perhaps the residents of Crested Butte took it for granted that every autumn during the slow tourist season, hundreds of cyclists would show up, but as other areas where such activities are possible began conducting their own versions of Fat Tire Bike Week, and in spite of its unsurpassed setting, Crested Butte began getting competition for the riders. After a significant decline in the number of riders and quality of activities organised by an overwhelmed volunteer staff, the local Chamber of Commerce stepped in to assist, and Fat Tire Bike Week has been to some extent reborn.

But with hundreds of riders taking part, most of them completely sober and equipped with the latest in mountain bike equipment, Fat Tire Bike Week will never be the same as my classic first ride over Pearl Pass in a group of only 13 people.

**Joe Breeze, the first mountain bike frame builder, riding Repack**

# CHAPTER 4

# The Coming of the Custom Bike

**A**s we have seen, a number of people contributed ideas or worked along similar lines independent of what was happening in the Bay Area in the seventies. If any single development brought mountain biking to the world, though, it was the construction of a bike frame built especially for multiple gear, fat-tyre bikes. As the limitations of the old bike frames became more and more apparent to those of us racing them, it seemed inevitable that someone would build a custom frame. Since most of us also had road bikes, the difference in quality was glaringly obvious, and if enough money was applied to the problem a custom clunker frame didn't seem out of the question. Long before anyone ever built one, custom off-road frames were the subject of interminable discussions, which always boiled down to who would be the first to convince a frame builder and put up the money, an opportunity that finally fell to me.

The first custom mountain bike frame that I know about was built for me in 1976 by a friend named Craig Mitchell. The idea was good, but the resulting frame didn't have the desired handling characteristics, so the bike was dis-assembled.

If any one person got the ball rolling, it was Joe Breeze. Joe was one of the Marin clunker group by virtue of a friend whose 1-speed clunker inspired Joe to buy an old used bike and refurbish it. Having done so, Joe was equipped with fairly standard clunker equipment, and his skills with it were reflected by the fact that he still holds the all-time second best time on Repack.

In one sense Joe was not like the other members of the clunker group: he was a skilled machinist and had taken Albert Eisentraut's bicycle frame building course. The pressure was still on for custom frames, and some time in 1977 I gave him a few hundred dollars and asked him if he would get started. Rumour spread fast, and in a short time, before he had welded a single tube, he had eight more orders. He decided to build ten bikes.

It took Joe a long time just to finish the design work. Because he was dealing with new design problems and trying so many new things, and because he is by nature a meticulous person, it was eight months from the first exchange of money to the delivery of my bike, the second (after Joe's) to be finished. Joe's personal bike now resides at the California Museum of Technology, in its own way as interesting a mechanical artefact as the first aeroplane, which, not at all coincidentally, was built by a pair of bicycle mechanics.

The bike as delivered had several features that have become standard on mountain bikes. Most significantly it had cantilever brakes rather than the drums used on clunkers. This reduced weight and permitted the use of high-quality hubs. The handlebars were flat motorcycle bars, and brake levers were Magura motorcycle (clutch and brake) levers. These served as the original standard on mountain bikes, and the brake levers now used were strongly influenced by them.

Breeze's bikes were limited in their performance by the rims and tyres then available. Subsequent manufacturing developments took several pounds off each wheel. The cantilever brakes were not very effective on the steel rims, especially in the wet.

For at least a year Joe Breeze's ten bikes were the only real mountain bikes in the Bay Area. In early 1979 a pair of Marin County brothers, Don and Erik Koski, introduced their own version of an off-roader, called the Trailmaster. Unfortunately, the design of the bike was far ahead of the Koski's ability to get it manufactured, and the bike was not a commercial success.

Concurrent with the development of his first off-road frames, Joe Breeze was involved in an attempt to set a tandem coast-to-coast record with his friend Otis Guy (Guy owns the third-best-ever Repack time). They had decided to have a young Bay Area frame builder named Tom Ritchey build their special bike.

Ritchey lived some 50 miles south of Marin, and for this reason he was only vaguely aware of the clunker movement going on there. Still, for years he had ridden his road bike on dirt roads and trails in the hills above his home in Palo Alto, and he had built for himself a bike based on the European 650-B tyre size that he used on the trails. In the course of designing the tandem, Joe showed Tom his mountain bike, and Ritchey was interested immediately.

Tom decided to build himself an off-road bike based on the 26-inch wheel. Because he thought he might as well see if anyone else wanted one, he built three rather than one. Ritchey's design took the Breeze bike as a starting point, but Tom added his ideas as well as Breeze's own impressions of what might be improved. The result, according to Ritchey, was not a radical departure in design from bikes that had existed for decades, although the use of balloon tyres with a derailleur gearing set up was unusual. As we have seen, bikes along the same lines had existed in the fifties, gears and all. The major difference between Tom Ritchey's bikes and those which preceded them was that Ritchey could make a lot of his, and the time was perfect for someone who wanted to do just that.

Having completed his first three mountain bike frames, Ritchey sold one to Gary Fisher, whom he had met when both raced road bikes. (Despite his local status as Repack record holder, Gary was still riding an old clunker, although Breeze had built his ten bikes a year earlier.) Fisher helped sell the other to a friend of his. At the same time, Gary had been talking with a Santa Rosa frame builder named Jeffrey Richman, who also built a pair of experimental mountain bikes that Gary helped sell to Marin County riders.

Getting one of Ritchey's first bikes wasn't a lot different from building a clunker. All that came from Ritchey was the frame, fork, handlebar, and bottom bracket, and it was up to the purchaser to select and assemble the equipment. The process still involved modifying equipment made to do something entirely different, and because the parts were purchased at retail prices in several different locations, the price was far above the range of the casual cyclist. Only a fanatic would spend over $1,000 to get what amounted to a bike kit.

About a month later Ritchey called Fisher and casually mentioned that he had in the meantime built another nine frames, in various sizes. Because the market for this kind of bike was better in Marin County than it was in Palo Alto, Ritchey asked Fisher if he wanted to help sell them.

At this point of the narrative I have to drop into the first person. Gary Fisher had been my room-mate while both of us discovered clunkers, and we had done much of our mechanical experimentation together. A little shocked by Ritchey's voluntary production, he came to me and asked if I would help him get rid of these bikes.

We scraped together a few hundred dollars and opened a checking account in the name of our new business, which we decided to call 'MountainBikes'. I am not sure who first called these bikes 'mountain bikes', and I was willing to give Joe Breeze the honour, which he rejected. He says that our commercial use was the first time he heard it, but I am certain that I heard the term when it was understood that it referred to a specific local mountain. An attempt to trademark that name was later rejected because of an administrative error in filing (an expensive error if there ever was one), and almost by default it has become the generic name for the bikes. Somehow the term ATB (for All-Terrain Bicycle) doesn't have nearly the romantic sound, and even where there are no mountains, people call them mountain bikes.

In its original form the arrangement was for Tom to build the frames, while Gary and I procured the parts, handled the assembly, and marketed the product. At first the entire process took place in each of our houses, and it required an enormous act of faith as well as disposable income to get one of our bikes. Because the business had virtually no capital, we required payment in full of $1,300 in advance; then we would go out and buy the parts and assemble the bike for delivery about a week later.

In the natural course of events we rented a shop and got down to the full-time business of making mountain bikes. As far as I can discover, this was the first commercial production of them.

The concept of mountain biking was not new by any means in 1979, since any number of people over the previous 100 years had ridden bicycles on roads as rough as any

**Top-notch road racer Tom Ritchey, inventor of the one-piece
bullmoose pattern handlebar, was already an established frame builder
when he teamed up with Gary Fisher and Charlie Kelly.**

we were used to. But the concept of off-road riding, coupled with bicycles of the quality of a fine road racer, was perfect for the times. Despite the scepticism on the part of the industry, bicyclists of all stripes accepted the new bikes as more than a fad.

More than anything, the ride convinced people. One gentleman came to our shop just to accompany a friend who was looking at bikes, and to let us know that he wasn't impressed by our bikes, he went on at length about his immaculate Cinelli. Finally, we talked him into taking a mountain bike for a spin around the block. He was gone for quite some time, and when he returned he wheeled the bike in with a sheepish look, saying, 'You know, this thing is very hard on prejudices'.

The first notice of the mountain bike movement in the press appeared in 1978 in a magazine published in Marin County, the *Co-Evolution Quarterly*, and the article had a significant impact. The writer, Richard Nilsen, lived part of the year in Colorado and part of the year in Marin County. While in Colorado he heard about the first Crested Butte to Aspen tour in 1976, and while in Marin he heard about the crazy Repack racers. Although at the time the groups had little in common, he linked them together in his article, called 'Clunker Bikes'.

When the article appeared, it was the first news the Californians and the Coloradans had of each other's accomplishments. It was this article that led five of us from Marin to arrange to go on the 1978 Pearl Pass tour, which in turn introduced the modern mountain bike to Crested Butte.

This leads to the interesting speculation that by spreading the awareness of the sport, the media had as much to do with the popularity of mountain biking as any mechanical development. In the next two years the bicycle press began to carry articles about mountain bikers, although few suggested that this was anything to take seriously. But for the sport to become popular, mass production had to be a part of the process. Various magazine articles detailed the expense and complications riders were willing to go through to get one of the few limited production mountain bikes, and perhaps it was this influence that turned the tide of industry indifference by suggesting that there really was a market for fat-tyre bikes.

The mountain bike phenomenon would not have gone anywhere unless bicycle manufacturers had gotten into the act by producing mass-produced bikes. But bicycle companies are conservative, and the idea of introducing an entirely new type of bike did not catch on easily.

The first manufacturer to look into the market was the Schwinn company. Since the clunker afficionados were buying large quantities of unusual bike parts from Schwinn dealerships to feed their off-road habits, company representatives took note. At about the same time in Southern California, the 'Beach Cruiser' craze was warming up. Cruisers were not like off-road clunkers; instead they were stripped-down 1-speed ballooners used by beach dwellers for local transportation around the level coastal towns.

Since balloon tyres seemed to be coming back, Schwinn brought out a new balloon-tyre model that displayed the Marin County influence in its name, the 'Clunker Five' (for five speeds) and its general set up including a tandem drum rear brake. The Clunker Five was a long way from the Marin County clunker standard, since it had a feeble calliper brake on the front, inadequate brake levers, and rubber pedals, but it showed that the industry was watching. Although no-one in Marin claimed ownership of the name 'Clunker', a few riders were somewhat miffed by this appropriation of the name, and said so in a letter to the Schwinn company. In a return letter a Schwinn attorney pointed out that the name had not been trademarked by anyone in Marin; however, with no other fanfare the name of the bike was changed in short order to the 'Spitfire Five'.

The Schwinn entry into the market didn't make many waves, especially since it was out-dated from the moment of its introduction. At the same time the Beach Cruiser had made an impact among BMX fans in Southern California, and the 'Cruiser Class' of 26- and 24-inch wheel bikes was becoming popular at BMX meets. Small BMX manufacturers began bringing out frames modelled after the old cantilever frames, but built from chrome-moly tubing. Clunker riders seized on these as the starting point for a new level of clunker construction, but except for the use of modern tubing, which saved several pounds, these bikes were not a great departure in design.

In January 1980, the first year that modern balloon-tyre bikes began appearing at the bicycle trade shows, there were four off-roaders on display at the Long Beach Bike Show. Of these, two were built on the BMX cruiser-style frame and only the Ritchey MountainBike and the Koski brothers' Trailmaster bike had diamond frames and looked like the modern version.

By the next year at the same bike show there were 15 manufacturers with their versions of mountain bikes, more and more commonly built on a diamond frame and similar to the Ritchey bike in design and choice of equipment. Surprisingly, some major manufacturers put their lack of vision on display by announcing pointedly in the cycling press that mountain bikes were a fad. Whatever the initial attitude, as it turned out all major bicycle companies now have mountain bikes in their catalogues.

In 1980 Specialized Bicycle Imports of San Jose, California, bought four of Ritchey's mountain bikes, which were used as the starting point for designing a mass-produced mountain bike. In 1981 Specialized introduced the Stumpjumper bicycle, which was very similar to the Ritchey, possibly setting the 'California Style' for mountain bikes. Other manufacturers followed suit within months, although much of the bike industry still refused to believe that mountain bikes were going anywhere.

During the same period when the bicycle manufacturers were catching on to the trend, components began appearing that helped the mountain bike movement considerably, starting in 1979 with the introduction of new rims and tyres. These were most likely inspired by the popularity of Cruiser Class BMX racing, because mountain bikes were not yet much of a force in the market place. Whatever the inspiration, these components were the last major breakthrough in the evolution of the mountain bike. Components have been refined since then, but nothing has been introduced since that time which has improved performance as much as lighter rims and tyres.

As the bikes evolved into a standard configuration, manufacturers started looking into componentry that was designed specifically for them, rather than attempting to adapt the components already available as clunker riders had done all along. The two giants of bicycle componentry, Shimano and SunTour, were sceptical at first, but paid close attention to the market, which threatened to explode from its grass roots just as BMX had. In the winter of 1982 both companies introduced component groups for mountain bikes, which included new designs of thumb-shifters and cantilever brakes, dirt-resistant hubs and bottom brackets, motorcycle-styled brake levers, and wide-range derailleurs.

The availability of component groups was the last stage of assembling the infra-structure necessary for mass production, and from that time forward mountain bike production swung into high gear, maintaining for several years the highest growth curve in the bicycle industry. For better or worse, mountain bikes were no longer a garage industry.

**Repack sagwagon**

# Racing before NORBA

Mountain bike competition began in 1976 with several events, the most well-known of which is the Repack Downhill described in the beginning of this book. The longest lived race, the Punk Bike Enduro, an underground event still held by invitation in a secret location somewhere in Northern California, also took place then, and in the same year in Crested Butte bored skiers frustrated by the lack of snow put on impromptu races for 'town bikes'. Also in 1976, a mountain bike pioneer in Chico, California, staged a ride for 'clunker', BMX and 10-speed bikes that became a de facto race. Clearly the urge to compete is an instinct that surfaces as soon as any form of human activity is developed or improved.

With no formal structure, races evolved for several years limited only by what people were willing to do on their mountain bikes. While the Repack event was a downhill, other races were cross-country, or in the case of the Punk Bike Enduro, stage races.

As it has expanded from an unstructured outlaw sport into an athletic challenge no more off-beat than cross-country ski racing, mountain bike racing has been sanitized to some extent in order for promoters to successfully market it to the masses. Certainly the idea of an event as loosely organised and uninsured as the Repack Downhill or the Punk Bike Enduro would strike terror into many hearts. But for those few of us who took part in those seminal events, there will never be an era like that again.

Nowadays mountain bike racers show up with their team jerseys and form-fitting Lycra shorts, wearing their special mountain bike racing shoes. They drive up in a team van; by contrast, many of the original Repack riders took a lift up the hill via a paved road in the back of a battered pink 1953 Chevrolet 1-ton dump truck. The joke about this particular truck was that it had failed the Mexican safety inspection.

**Line-up for first cross-country race, Marin County, 1977: Fred Wolf · Wende (**
**Gary Fisher · Joe Breeze · Eric Fletcher · Craig Mit**

At each race dozens of riders took their lives in their hands, piling machines and selves high in the back and dangling off the sides while the truck ground slowly up the mountain.

The very first cross-country mountain bike race I know about took place in the autumn of 1977, just before Joe Breeze delivered the first of his custom bikes. My room-mate, Alan Bonds, and I promoted the race and laid out the course in the hills near the Repack course. We rounded up a crew of about two dozen to race, and the photograph we took just before we pushed off is a classic. It shows sixteen riders lined up, with only one or two exceptions all on similarly modified old bikes featuring drum brakes, 'fork braces' and wide handlebars. In the centre of the picture Gary Fisher balances on his bike with his hands on Joe Breeze's and my shoulders. Several riders wear T-shirts with a logo reading 'Marin County Klunkers'.

In a chequered bicycle racing career both on road and off, I had few chances to win races. But it was easier to be good in a sport that had only three or four serious contenders. In this race I charged to the front with two others, and as they faded, I realised the race was mine to win. I had no sooner completed the thought, when I ran smack into one of the typical problems we all had with our jury-rigged bikes. My drum brake cable came loose where it had been taped to the chain stay, the crank arm snagged it, and I came to a sliding, cursing stop. As I struggled with the problem a spectator handed me a piece of twine, an act that would be illegal under modern

k Lindlow·Robert Stewart·Chris Lang·Jim Preston·Ian Stewart·Charles Kelly
Drumm·Roy Rivers·Alan Bonds·Unidentified

mountain bike race rules. I hastily tied up the cable and got back under way, now in about seventh place. And on a course that I had laid out myself, I got lost. It's amazingly easy to ride right past a junction without seeing it when your head is down and sweat is running in your eyes. I wound up riding an extra four or five miles, conceding the race in very unsportmanlike manner to Alan, my surprised roommate.

While the mountain bike scene was building in Marin County, a former Olympic bike racer who was born with the name Michael Hiltner but who had during the turbulent sixties changed it to 'Victor Vincente of America' was leading the mountain bike movement in Southern California. Victor, who prefers to be called by either his first name or the entire handle, including '. . . of America', had been working on his own designs for off-road bicycles, and had come to a conclusion shared by several other designers of the period, i.e., that the 20-inch wheels and tyres made for BMX bikes were far superior to those made at that time for 26-inch balloon-tyre bikes.

Because BMX had blossomed into a major part of the bike industry by the mid-seventies, manufacturers were falling all over themselves to develop the lightest and strongest rims and tyres for 20-inch wheels. Clunker riders had rejected BMX bikes as too small and cramped for a 6-plus-footer to take on an extended cross-country ride, but the light wheels and superior tyres appealed to some as a solution to the weight problem caused by the obsolete steel 26-inch rims and Uniroyal tyres.

Victor's approach was the 'Topanga' bike, a multiple-geared off-roader with a full-size frame and 20-inch wheels. This design saved considerable weight, although the rider paid a penalty for the smaller diameter wheels with a rougher ride. With his light bike and his years of cycling experience, Victor was just about unbeatable in the climbs, although his descending would not threaten a Repack rider.

The first of the two dozen or so Topanga bikes that Victor built over the next three years was ready about the end of 1979, shortly after Tom Ritchey's frames came on the market. By this time the information network was beginning to spread among those interested in off-road bikes, and those of us in the Bay Area 400 miles north heard of Victor just in time to attend his first mountain bike race, the first running of the 'Reseda-to-the-Sea' in March 1980.

One of the members of the Northern California off-road bike scene was a wealthy and somewhat eccentric man named John Finley Scott, who had made his money in investments while holding down a professor's chair at the University of California. As mentioned elsewhere, Scott had in 1953 constructed what he called a 'woodsy bike' that was strikingly similar to a modern mountain bike, and in 1979 he invested some money into a struggling concern, the trinity of Tom Ritchey, Gary Fisher, and myself doing business as MountainBikes, the first commercial production of off-roaders.

Among other vehicles, Scott owned a double-decker London bus, repainted in a sort of Green Line livery to blend with the surroundings. The bus had been extensively refurbished to act as a support vehicle for extended bike tours. All the seats had been removed from the lower level, and bike hooks were installed on the ceiling. Some of the upper seats had also been removed to make room for luggage and sleeping space. The original engine had been replaced by a Cummins diesel that made so much noise in the driver's compartment that the driver wore airport noise protectors over his ears while driving. With the bottom layer festooned with bikes, passengers enjoyed the view from high above traffic.

On the occasion of the first Reseda-to-the-Sea, several of his acquaintances prevailed on Scott to take a load of riders to it. Accordingly a dozen of us loaded bikes and selves into the bus for the late-night run south.

Although the Northern California clunker scene at that time involved several hundred riders, and races had been going on for over three years, this was the first event held in Southern California. Accordingly, about thirty-five locals turned out, including a couple of well-known road racers on cyclo-cross bikes. They were shocked and awestruck to see a busload of riders from far away, riders who already displayed a considerable level of organisation with their bus and quite a few custom bikes. They marvelled at the fact our group included several women riders, since at that time female mountain bikers did not exist in Southern California.

The Northern Californians lived up to their reputations by sweeping the results, although Southerner Ron Skarin finished second on a cyclo-cross bike. The course included so much paved surface and smooth dirt roads that all the cyclo-crossers had charged into the lead, only to run into wheel problems on the fast and rough descent.

Gary Fisher took the top prize that day, beginning a string of victories that over the next few years would make him the hottest rider on the infant racing circuit. The awarding of a Topanga bike for first place marked the biggest race prize to date, the first time a bike had been a prize in a mountain bike race.

For those who were used to a certain amount of production, the first and subsequent Reseda races were remarkably free of rules and any other impediments to fun. Riders gathered at an intersection in Reseda, as traffic continued to flow around the knot of bikers. No one really gave the starting command, but when the group reached a critical mass, everyone headed up the road. The distance was short, about 12 miles, and quite a bit of that was on asphalt, a far cry from the more rugged conditions riders came to demand from races.

There was some debate at the Reseda race about whether the racing should go in the direction of cyclo-cross. Mountain bikers from the Repack school didn't care to have anything to do with the skinny-tyre version of cross-country, and Skarin's second place at Reseda rubbed a few the wrong way. Another Southern California cyclo-crosser named Clark Roberts started showing up at subsequent races and placing respectably. Late in 1980 Gary Fisher returned the favour by placing second at the Northern California Cyclo-cross championships on his mountain bike, thanks to the recent introduction of lighter aluminium rims.

One possible way to keep cyclo-cross bikes out of mountain bike races would be by establishing a minimum tyre width requirement. But mountain bikers saw racing as a way to improve the bike, and it seemed contrary to that spirit to restrict what people could ride. Of course, the cyclo-cross bikes were not as rugged as mountain bikes, even if they were considerably lighter, so promoters responded by putting together courses that were certain to destroy cyclo-cross wheels with high-speed, rough descents. When the first discussions were held concerning appropriate national mountain bike rules, the situation was addressed by a rule that requires competitors to finish on the original equipment without any outside support, just as the recreational rider must presumably do on the same equipment.

Cyclo-cross riders are used to disposable bicycles and wheels, and with the aid of a pit crew they often switch from one bike to another in mid-race. By making the rider self-reliant, the mountain bike rules also attempted to keep the racing egalitarian by preventing the availability of massive support to the professional from giving him an advantage over the independent rider.

Another of the early races on the California circuit was the Central Coast Clunker Classic held in the hills above San Luis Obispo from 1980 to 1983. Half-way between the Bay Area and Los Angeles, the Classic was one of the few races that drew appreciable numbers from both ends of the state. This event was promoted by Glenn Odell, who went on to become the first owner of the national sanctioning organisation (NORBA) shortly after it was formed in 1983. Like the other races of the time, the now-defunct Clunker Classic was low-key. Riders assembled in a campground where they were also expected to sleep. Because this was before hundreds of people started showing up at every race, numbers were manageable, and when all the bikers found themselves camped together, the inevitable two-day party started.

The course was about 30 miles through the hills of the Coast Range, and it included a couple of dozen stream crossings that were up to several feet deep, requiring the rider to wade across in cold, thigh-deep water which was so refreshing that some riders abandoned reasonable placings to go swimming.

The Central Coast Clunker Classic was the first mountain bike event to fall victim to the reaction by others to the presence of mountain bikes. After four runnings of the Classic, the land which the course crossed was made out of bounds to bicycles, ending the series.

## Underground at the Punk Bike Enduro

Because it is unique and has endured through all the phases of mountain bikes and biking, the Punk Bike Enduro, or PBE as it is known to the invitees, deserves a little illumination. The race started in 1975, before mountain bikes even came on the scene, as a challenge between cyclo-cross riders and the BMX rats who shared the same Northern California shop space. Since that time the cyclo-cross influence has disappeared and the BMX influence has been absorbed by mountain bikes, and the PBE has become a mountain bike race more or less by default.

In order to protect its underground status and to keep the number of riders manageable, the Enduro is not announced publicly. When the social pressure builds to a critical point, one or another of the casual PBE 'directors' will organise a race. Selecting a time and place, he calls a couple of dozen riders who have been arbitrarily chosen to take part, usually all his pals along with a couple of out-of-towners who have enough friends in the chosen group to get the word.

The PBE is a stage race, but the BMX influence at its roots keeps the stages short; the longest is usually under 2 miles. Riders assemble at the assigned starting spot, where the race director tells them what the course will be for the stage. Because the stages are short, there is little chance of a rider getting lost. It's hard to get lost when you're sprinting madly down a road elbow-to-elbow with a dozen others. The short stages keep the pace of the Enduro up to maximum velocity, and as the pack flies down the rough road, only the leaders can see what they are about to ride over. The result of this activity would not thrill an insurance statistician; riders go down, sometimes in groups, and bikes suffer an amazing amount of damage for the distance covered.

As soon as all the riders have finished a stage and have had a few minutes to catch their breath, the race director announces the route for the next stage, which usually but not always starts at the ending point of the previous stage.

The scoring is handled by a point system, since timing this madness would be out of the question. There are anywhere from a dozen to twenty stages. Each rider is awarded points representing his stage finishes, one point for each first, two points for each second, and so on. At the end of the event the rider with the lowest score wins. As an example of how casual the planning for the Enduro is, riders have been known to rebel and refuse to follow the director's plan. One race director swears that the whole idea behind the race is to drive the riders to revolt, and it wouldn't be a complete Enduro without a revolution.

Despite the casual organisation, the competition at the PBE is at least as fierce as any on the professional circuit, probably fiercer, because the only rules in effect are related solely to the scoring, and even if there were rules, there isn't anyone to enforce them. The professional off-road races favour strength and climbing ability, but the Punk Bike Enduro rewards sheer aggression coupled with a good sprint. While the pro off-road riders must pace themselves, no such limitation applies for the Punkers. Whatever exact qualities among the riders this race selects for, it finds them fast, and the group will start shedding riders by the third stage.

Bicycle damage is a major factor, and this is the reason that cyclo-cross bikes have disappeared from the race. Early in the going the cyclo-crossers found that they had a higher top speed than any of the other bikes, but the inevitable flat tyres and wheel damage were too costly.

Like the Repack races, the PBE doesn't feature a lengthy prize list, and for the participants, doing well is the best reward. The Punk Bikers and some outlaw racers are the last of the throw-backs to the more carefree days of mountain bike competition. They have no desire to take their sport any farther than it has already gone; it is enough for them, and who cares what the rest of the world thinks? They don't deal with a league, insurance, or sanction specifications. The sport is rough, and competitors have lost their share of skin along with suffering a few more serious injuries, but that is considered part of the challenge. No-one is there who has not decided to accept that challenge, and no-one pretends to take responsibility for the riders' safety.

Of course, no sponsor would ever touch an event like the Punk Bike Enduro. Many people would not consider this type of activity 'good for the sport', since it could give the impression that the participants are a group of environmental rapists bent on pillaging the forest for their own enjoyment. The Punk Bikers don't see themselves this way, since the Enduro is a once-a-year activity not necessarily reflective of their riding during the rest of the year. However, it is clear that the Enduro is not likely to join the mainstream of society as a form of mountain bike competition and that is as it should be. The world still needs this end of the sport, but on this level it could never be presented to more than a few dozen people at any time.

**Joe Murray, NORBA's first US Men's Champion**

# Competition:
# A Crash Course

In contrast to the cavalier attitude of the Punk Bikers and early Repack riders, concern for the riders' safety is now one of the key factors at the heart of the development of the sport mountain bike racing as it is presented to the general public. Today in Europe and the U.S. mountain bike racing is starting to attract television coverage and corporate sponsors. On both sides of the Atlantic, World Championships have been held and the grip that U.S. pro's once had on the sport is being loosened by riders like the UK's Tim Gould, one of many road racers now converting to off-road racing. It is the latest development in a chain of events that goes back to the early Eighties when, with mountain bike events mushrooming all over the place, promoters and racers felt pressure to combine their efforts in the areas of insurance and rules.

This meant the development of some form of governing body. The result was the formation in 1983 in the U.S. of the National Off-Road Bicycle Association (NORBA). NORBA held its first meeting at my house on January 25, 1983. The interest among the group of only 13 people was sufficient that the second meeting was held only two days later, as the founding members began charting out a set of standard off-road rules. Although more rules have been added since then in response to new problems, these remain the core of the current rule book and have influenced the development of the sport in every country. Much of the UK's first rulebook, where a separate and independent NORBA was started in 1984 was based on those efforts.

NORBA UK, slightly ahead of its time and subject to various false starts, failed to attract the sort of support necessary to maintain a full-time organisation and no longer exists, its leading role in the sport now assumed by its successor, the Mountain Bike Club.

Nonetheless what NORBA UK did achieve is worth recording because it helped establish the mood, spirit and much of the format of mountain bike racing in this country as it borrowed and adapted ideas from its US counterpart.

NORBA UK staged the first mountain bike race on a short 1.25 mile course at Eastway Cycle Centre in East London in 1984. Nobody for one moment imagined that tearing round this modified urban cyclo-cross course was how mountain bike racing was intended to be. Cyclo-cross courses like Eastway and motorbike motocross courses are sometimes still used by promoters keen to attract novice riders to the sport. Short urban circuits are satisfactory insofar as they are conveniently located, and allow crowds to follow all the action. From a racer's point of view they're repetitious, unadventurous and deprive you of an opportunity to enjoy the countryside. All this was quickly apparent to the UK's pioneering organiser Tim Gartside, who in conjunction with *Bicycle Action* magazine, then launched the UK's first series of races the Fat Tyre Five. Each was unique in terms of course, structure and location; Tim, one of life's natural enthusiasts, managed to persuade landowners in some of the country's choicer and remoter beauty spots, the Black Mountains, the Yorkshire Dales and the Quantocks, that breathtaking mountain bike racing and breathtaking countryside had much to offer each other, projecting the vision of mountain bike racing as an ultra-modern rural sport.

Nowhere was this vision better put into effect than in mid-Wales, where the Hay Classic, beginning near Hay-on-Wye, quickly became a landmark event. With a course that climbed steeply over sheep-grazed moorlands in the Black Mountains before making plunging descents down forest fireroads to the valley floor, it brought the Outward Bound element to mountain biking. So rugged was the course that marshals in Land Rovers had to be posted on some of the peaks to prevent stragglers becoming lost in the mist. The Hay Classic struck a chord and would probably still be a premier race but for an even more outrageous opportunity that came along to give mountain bike racing in the UK its highest profile event.

## Man versus Horse

Twenty miles west of Hay, in Llantrwyd Wells on the edge of the Brecon Beacons, publican Gordon Green, had, so the PR legend now goes, heard two customers arguing over whether a man was equal to a horse over a significant distance. Gordon, in the hope of injecting some life (and some visitors) into an Edwardian spa resort that had seen better days decided to put the argument to the test.

The first Man v Horse race was held in June 1980 with a horse beating the runner by 43 minutes. Two years later the 22-mile course, which now has climbs totalling over 4,000 feet, was modified to make it a more even match, but a horse still won by four minutes. In 1985 Gordon Green, seeing the potential in mountain bikes, had no hesitation in throwing open the Man v Horse challenge to mountain bike riders. With the sponsors, bookmakers William Hill, offering 50–1 odds and offering £4,000 to the first mountain bike rider to beat the horse, the race quickly attracted professional U.S. riders, then the only paid and experienced pro's on the scene. The first race with mountain bikes competing was run on a warm June day with U.S. women's champion Jackie Phelan coming in 27 minutes behind the horse and one minute behind the runner. The next year, in wet and muddy conditions American Roy Rivers came in 33 minutes behind the horse and even further behind the runner.

In the horse and running camps it looked as if the much-vaunted mountain bike wasn't all it claimed to be. What those camps failed to realise was that with every year mountain bikes were becoming more state of the art. Each year brought changes. As the bikes improved so did the riders. More people were piling into the sport as more cycle manufacturers added mountain bikes to their ranges. In 1988 Peugeot UK decided to promote its mountain bike range by giving production models to its cyclo-cross team. Its leader, Tim Gould, had already won British cyclo-cross's classic, the gruelling Three Peaks race, five times. Probably one of the toughest roughstuff races in the world, it covers 35 miles of fells with competitors riding and carrying their bikes to the top of the three peaks, Whernside, Pen-y-Ghent and Ingleborough. For Tim the 22-mile Man v Horse circuit was no worse than a gruelling training run.

In 1988 on a dry, warm day he came within five minutes of the horse and became the first cyclist to beat a runner. The event, with competing communities of cyclists, runners and horsefolk is atmosphere rich, and, among the crowds who follow it, the betting was that Tim, now he knew the course, could beat a horse, especially if the weather was hot – conditions the horses like least. In 1989, the race was held on one of the hottest days of the year. Tim Gould finished in 1 hour 51 minutes and 26 seconds, the fastest horse took three minutes more, Gould collected a £5,000 cheque and mountain bike history was made.

## The Race Scene

Man v Horse is one of a number of unusual one-off races that pepper the annual mountain bike race calendar. Following the early NORBA tradition they are put on by organisers keen to attract mountain bike riders to areas of natural beauty, and the ride more than the race is often the reason for taking part. Details about these can usually been garnered from any of the magazines dedicated to the sport.

The flavour of the race scene continues to vary. At one extreme there are still the essentially funky events of mountain biking's early days where it's the ride that counts. At the other end is the emerging track scene, borrowing some of its influences, livery and attitudes from the various worlds of cyclo-cross, road racing, BMX racing and even motocross. This is the competitive end, the sharp end where winning counts and losing hurts.

The UK's two current sanctioning bodies are the Mountain Bike Club, which now organises the de facto UK Championships and its rival, the British Mountain Bike Association.

Their rules are roughly similar, based on the fundamental principle of off-road competition requiring a rider to be self-sufficient. A mountain bike rider must be able to keep his bike running under ordinary mountain biking circumstances. In contrast to the rules for racing road bicycles, mountain bike rules make the racer responsible for his own repairs. Ever since the days of Repack and the Punk Bike Enduro, riders realised that racing was the quickest way to find out about equipment, what worked and what didn't, but more important, what held up and what didn't. The rules were designed to encourage this trend. Because there are no limits on the type of equipment competitors may use as long as it works, mountain bike racing spurs practical development in a way that road racing does not.

Nothing stays simple forever, and races now are likely to be gatherings of several hundred racers and even more spectators. Competitors are divided into a half-dozen categories including a professional class in slick uniforms; this is a long way from the jeans-and-boots crowd. The only safety requirement is that some form of hard-shell helmet is worn—the traditional banana-shaped road-racing helmet is no longer deemed to provide adequate protection.

A further development on the racing scene is the diversity of events. There are now cross-country races, stage races, observed trials, and in spite of some social pressure, there are still downhill races. Each type of event has different requirements regarding rules, and rulebooks are getting thicker. For example, the reasonably simple require-ment that riders must wear helmets is complicated because helmets must then be defined. Insurance companies take this area very seriously, and since without insurance there would be no racing, the desires of the insurance company statisticians must be taken into account in the rules.

Suddenly, mountain bike racing is important to some people and their approach is no longer carefree. The manufacturer who sponsors a team wants to see well-run events with a maximum of publicity. The promoter wants an unimpeachable set of rules that are simple and easily applied, but the nature of competition is such that with so many people looking for the winning edge, grey areas are continually cropping up.

If rules are created for every possible problem, racing can turn into bureaucracy. Here is an example of the type of situation that gives race promoters fits. At one race a rider snapped his chain just after the start, and retired to the starting area where he repaired the damage. Restarting from the line, he passed most of the field and eventually placed second. Complications arose when other riders protested that he had received outside help when he borrowed a chain tool in the starting area; the rider felt that since he had repaired the damage before riding the entire distance, his repair had taken place before he started. Obviously the rider in question put in a magnificent ride to do as well as he did but depending on the interpretation he may have stretched the rules in the process. This matter was appealed, and several different decisions were rendered depending on who was appealing. The unfortunate result of the conflict was that the promoter decided that he had had enough of mountain bike race promotion, and the area lost a formerly enthusiastic promoter.

Rule interpretations only affect those at the top of the field. The majority of the participants at the average race don't come with the intention of cashing in on their athletic skills. For these people mountain bike racing is, like cross-country skiing or running races, a means of challenging themselves. At the Mountain Bike Club's six-round National championships participants run into the hundreds, most of whom are average riders rather than fierce competitors.

The high turnout at national and local events reflects how unintimidating mountain bike racing is compared to novice road racing. Road racers must learn to ride in large packs, and for a new racer this can be frightening, especially in the novice categories where crashes are more frequent than in the pro classes. Road racing demands experience just for the rider to get into it, while mountain bike racing can be enjoyable for a rider with no previous experience. Because road racers live and die by the 'draft', or wind resistance, they must ride in groups, and the tactics and strategy and team work of road racing are complex. Mountain bike racing is more of a test of strength and skill than it is of tactics and team work.

One trend in off-road racing is toward short lap courses. These make sense for some reasons, ease of control, spectators, sponsorship, and so on. Ideal places for mountain bike races are reasonably limited, if 'ideal' is 20–40 miles of winding dirt road and trail through mountains and forests. Unfortunately, short lap courses aren't as much fun for a rider to continue on after the pack has gone up the road, or worse, when the leaders lap for the third time. Sponsors press for shorter courses because mountain bike races can be more easily presented as entertainment for non-participants. Most racers would probably prefer to race on longer courses, point-to-point on an interesting route.

The reason to race may not even be just to race but to be there after the race. Equipment freaks go wild at races inspecting whatever the local garage mechanics have come up with. Anyone who wants to learn about mountain bikes should attend a race, because the conversation among however many riders there are will not cover many other subjects.

## Observed Trials

One branch of mountain bike competition has become an entity unto itself: observed trials. The contest of skill is as much a natural direction in competition as the contest of speed. The special requirements of this sport have brought about the development of bikes that have limited applications for the general mountain bike rider, and in that sense they are not really mountain bikes. However, since observed trials are becoming standard at some two-day events to determine pole position for the next day's race it can pay to hone your skills in this department.

Depending on the rules of the competition, riders may be required to ride the same bike in all stages of an extended contest. Modifications to the bike, specifically removal of the large chainrings for the trials stage, is not always permitted. In a contest of observed trials only, competitors will use bikes with special characteristics which permit performance that can't be duplicated on a standard mountain bike.

Such special bikes will have a shorter wheelbase, high bottom bracket, and steep head angle, all built on the smallest possible frame. Most also include a skid plate under the chainring to prevent damage to it and to keep the bike from hanging up on obstacles.

### Observed Trials: the art is total control

Because the use of smaller diameter wheels permits shorter wheelbases, 20- and 24-inch wheels are common, and some frames feature two sizes of wheels. The saddle on a trials bike is there as a matter of form only, because it is rarely used.

Observed trials are an outgrowth of motorcycle trials where skill in bike handling rather than speed is the essential element. Just about every mountain biker has approached an obstacle at one time or another and attempted to ride over or around it without stopping. Observed trials are simply structured competitions based around obstacles.

Trials are scored in the manner of golf, i.e. the rider with the lowest score is the winner. The course is laid out as a series of specific problems, called traps, which may be from a few yards to 50 or 60 feet in length. The sides of the traps are marked by coloured tape, and the object is for the competitor to ride from one end to the other without putting down a foot. The rule is 'front wheel in, front wheel out', which means that the rider is scored from the time the front axle crosses the start to when it crosses the finish. If the rider completes the trap without putting down a foot, it is called a 'clean' ride, that is, no score or zero. The worst score on a trap is a five, a failure, which is awarded if the rider falls, rides outside the boundaries, refuses to ride the trap, or comes to a complete stop with one or both feet on the ground. Each 'dab', or foot on the ground not accompanied by a full stop, is scored as one point up to the third dab. After the third point, if the rider finishes the trap without a complete failure for five points, the score is three points.

The standards of judging vary considerably from one set of observed trials to another and even between traps at the same contest, because the scoring is open to quite a bit of interpretation, such as the definition of a full stop. One judge may see it one way, and a judge at another trap at the same contest may see it differently. This usually has a minimal effect on the score since each judge's interpretation will apply equally to all riders, but occasionally riders will become confused when there are dramatic differences between judges.

Trials rules prevent the competitor from practising on the course, although walking a trap without the bike is permitted. Since obstacles for the highest level of trials verge on the impossible, the promoter must be able to prove at any time that a trap is possible by having a rider of his choice demonstrate it. Of course, the promoter's demonstrator may have spent the previous afternoon practising the obstacle, an advantage over a rider attempting it for the first time.

Obstacles for observed trials can be as simple as a few rocks or logs scattered on a trial, a situation familiar to most mountain bikers, or as a profound as riding over a car. The latter is a situation only rarely faced by the average mountain biker, and at this extreme, observed trials is more an acrobatic act than anything to do with mountain bike riding. A good trials rider commands the bike as an extension of the body; required skills include riding off a 4-foot drop, making a 180-degree pivot on either wheel, and riding over obstacles several feet high.

Trials riding may be a departure from mountain biking at its highest expression, but there is no sharp delineation between the two, such as the difference between BMX and mountain biking. At its simplest, trials is a group of mountain bikers on a recreational outing attempting to ride up the legendary hill without putting down a foot, or seeing who can get the farthest. This type of trials isn't formal, but it's fundamental and instinctive. Most experienced mountain bikers pride themselves on their skills in picking routes through difficult terrain.

Because observed trials don't require large tracts of land, and can even be staged in a carpark (quite a departure from mountain biking!), promoters find this event attractive. From the stand-point of spectators, trials are nearly perfect, since all the action, and there is plenty, takes place in a confined area, unlike that of a mountain bike race.

# Off-Road Touring

One area where mountain bikes are becoming a major factor is touring. The reasons are obvious: mountain bikes are considerably more resistant to damage than ordinary 10-speed touring bicycles, and under touring conditions the difference in average speed between a narrow-tyre bike and a mountain bike with the tyres inflated to 80 psi is insignificant, especially if the mountain bike is equipped with road-type fat tyres. The ruggedness and versatility of the mountain bike more than make up for any limitations in speed for road touring. Of course, the mountain bike introduces the possibility of touring in extremely remote areas and on poor road surfaces.

In a few short years tourists on mountain bikes have already penetrated the Himalayas, the Andes, and the Amazon Basin. I have taken my bike to the subarctic, and the Crane cousins of England have taken theirs to the top of Kilimanjaro. Mountain bike riders have crossed the Sahara and explored the remotest regions of China. There is virtually no limit to the areas the mountain biker can visit, and for that reason I believe that for many people now living in out-of-the-way places the first impression of our culture will come from tourists on mountain bikes.

To some extent the popularity of the mountain bike is the return to a previously established precedent. In what is sometimes referred to as the Third World, the bicycle has always been a dominant form of transportation. But the long history of the bicycle includes its use as an important means of transportation in the Yukon and Alaska Territories during the great Gold Rush that took place just as the first major 'Bike Boom' was reaching its frenzied peak. During the winter in these areas the frozen rivers served as bicycle highways, and according to their own accounts at least two different bicyclists made the 1,000-mile ride from Dawson in the Yukon down the

**Heading for home after a long day in the saddle**

frozen Yukon River to Nome on the west coast of Alaska, both in the year 1900. Contemporary news accounts suggest that bicycles were a frequent if not regular sight on the famous trail from Skagway to Dawson.

In comparison to such epic journeys my own mountain bike touring experience seems pretty tame, but keep in mind that the men who undertook these incredible rides were prospecting for gold, a quest that frequently drives men to feats that are better left untried. Considering that in both of the Yukon River accounts the riders had several life-threatening experiences, perhaps there were others who attempted the same ride and died en route.

Modern bicycle touring is usually a little more recreational than a trip down the frozen Yukon, and even mountain bike touring can be remarkably civilised. The Crested Butte-Pearl Pass tour probably qualifies as the first indicator of a major trend in mountain bike touring. Although the format has since changed, originally the idea was that a group of mountain bikers could take a tour in a superb area, while the camping gear and food were hauled in a few 4-wheel drive vehicles. The concept isn't that new, since this was similar to a practice already in use among road cyclists, but the off-road application was perhaps even a better application. The burden of panniers and gear is enough to limit off-road performance, and given the choice riders are just as happy to let someone else carry the supplies so they can more completely enjoy the recreational aspects of the ride.

The problem with the Pearl Pass tour was that it in time it became such a popular event that the logistics became impossible as the number of riders swelled to several hundred.

Since then dozens of tour promoters large and small have picked up on the same idea and applied it in a more easily controlled manner to mountain bike tours. As long as the group of riders is kept within reason, one vehicle can easily haul the supplies. The same vehicle can act as a sweep or sagwagon, or go ahead so someone can start cooking dinner and setting up camp.

This is the pattern followed by many of the professional mountain bike touring out-fits, but of course the possibilities created by the mountain bike lend themselves to a variety of group tour arrangements, ranging from luxury tours in which lodging is in hotels and the sagwagon carries all the supplies, to the other end of the spectrum, with riders carrying their own supplies and camping out each night. Prices for guided tours run accordingly, from a few dollars a day to as much as a hundred for hotel-to-hotel tours.

Most tour operators offer different levels of tours, with options including bicycle and helmet rentals or rental of camping equipment.

On less formally supported tours, riders will have to cope with carrying their own equipment. The weight of a fully loaded touring bike puts a burden on the bike's wheels, and for this reason the fatter tyres and wider rims of the mountain bike give it a huge margin of strength and control over a road touring bike. The mountain bike rider doesn't worry as much when he is forced off the paved roads onto the gravel shoulder by a logging truck; the wheels won't collapse and the bike won't go out of control.

# Touring Equipment

The items the rider brings on any particular tour must be chosen with an eye to what the tour entails. For more rugged tours the rider may have to carry enough supplies to survive under desperate conditions, while the overnight tourist can travel with a light load. With one exception, what you bring is not so important as how you carry it on the bike.

The one important consideration for all tours and rides in general is warm clothing and rain gear if rain is likely. If you wear too much, you can always take some off, but if you didn't bring it you can't put it on if you're cold or if it's raining. A down jacket doesn't weigh much, and it's cheap insurance.

Let's get back to how the gear is put on the bike. For reasons of control, and especially if the bike has to be carried, it's a good idea to balance the load from front to rear. If this is not done it can be difficult to pick the severely imbalanced bike up. A frame pad or shoulder sling makes the bike a lot easier to carry.

Weight distribution has a pronounced effect on the bike's handling. If the front is lightly loaded, or if the weight on the rear is too far back, the front end feels light and hard to control on rough ground.

'Low riding' front panniers are popular among bicycle tourists because they keep the bike's centre of gravity low, and by balancing the weight of the front panniers around the axis of the steering, they reduce the inertia that resists steering. Because of the design differences between mountain bikes and road bikes, manufacturers have come up with special designs of low riding racks for fat-tyre bikes. In general these carry the load a little higher than low riding racks made for road bikes, because if the panniers are too low they can catch on rocks or brush, a problem that doesn't usually affect a road rider.

In order to avoid wear on the panniers and control problems from brush and rocks, some mountain bike tourists suggest that the front gear be carried in the time-honoured position above the front wheel that it occupied before the designers got hold of the problem.

Mountain bike tourists now have their choice of rear racks designed for off-road bikes. In general these will be a little beefier than road racks, and most also double as a rear mudguard when the bike isn't loaded. The key to the touring racks front and rear is that the gear must not interfere with the brakes. Since there are so many braking options on the market, this may or may not be a problem.

Speaking of racks as mudguards, these are another fairly standard touring option for road bikes. Depending on where the mountain biker is going, mudguards can be a problem if the wheel picks up a lot of mud. The rear rack will deflect most of the muck from the rear wheel. In front a common option is a small plastic flap attached to the down tube, positioned to deflect the mud that would hit the rider in the face.

**Winter in Wales sometimes you have to make your own trail**

**Deep in the Yukon—The Canol Road, abandoned as soon as
it was built**

# The Arctic Cycle

Having heard of the adventures of people conquering remote goals such as the Himalayas, Kilimanjaro, and Mont Blanc via mountain bike, I have always felt a twinge of jealousy for those who embark on these historic firsts. Despite being in on the beginning of the movement, my mountain bike riding has been mostly confined to civilized parts of the world. I finally had my chance to put my tyre tracks where no bicycle had ever been, when six of us cycled Canada's Canol Road just 200 miles south of the Arctic Circle in the rugged tundra and mountains of the Far North.

When the lure of gold first drew prospectors to the Yukon at the turn of the century, the first 'bike boom' had just inspired a frenzy of cycling activity in the continental United States. As far back as 1884 Thomas Stevens had completed the first coast-to-coast bicycle trip, through largely roadless and uncharted territory, proving the bicycle's ability in rugged terrain.

In the Yukon in 1900, winter travel was normally by means of dog sled. But that meant that the traveller had to feed his dogs, and he had to find a place to keep them, a real problem in the camps where the dogs' idle time was spent in tearing each other apart. It is not surprising then that many of the miners took to bicycles as their winter form of transportation, since the frozen rivers provided excellent routes.

The only assurance we had that the road we were to ride had never been bicycled was the fact that it was built long after the Gold Rush and abandoned almost immediately. The Canol Road was built at enormous expense and hardship during World War II to supply oil from Norman Wells, which was at the time the northern-most producing oilfield in the Western Hemisphere, to Whitehorse some 600 miles away. By the time the construction was completed, the strategic elements that caused it to be built had changed, and it was abandoned only a few months after the first barrel of oil arrived in Whitehorse.

While the part of the Canol Road that lies within the Yukon Territory is maintained and is still used as the major route northeast of Whitehorse, 200 miles of the Canol that lie within the wild and rugged Northwest Territories (NWT) have now been unmaintained for four decades and are impassable to motor traffic. It sounded perfect for mountain bikes, both as a ride in magnificent country and as a means to explore one of the most remote areas in North America.

Two days of air travel and another entire day in a 4-wheel-drive vehicle took us to our jumping-off point. The last outpost that can be reached by vehicle from Whitehorse is Oldsquaw Lodge, a summer observation post on the tundra for naturalists studying the unique flora and fauna of the region. In August the birds have shed their brilliant mating plumage and the wildflowers have bloomed, so in 1985 the operators of Oldsquaw, Nancy Eagleson and Sam Miller, decided to experiment with a mountain bike tour on the Canol. Accordingly, six of us, three men and three women, pushed off on a brilliantly clear day, bikes loaded with gear, for the first ever mountain bike ride in the road's 40-year history. Our crew consisted of Americans Wendy Lippman, Al Farrell, and myself, plus Canadians Anne Mullens and Tony Carson, guided by Nancy Eagleson, who was 'born in the U.S.A' but is now a resident of Canada.

It would be hard to find a more dissimilar group of individuals than our crew, who had little in common with each other except an interest in mountain bikes. Because of this and the fact that most of us were strangers to each other, the ride was as much an exercise in group dynamics as it was a mountain bike tour. Al was a municipal bond salesman from Beverly Hills, Anne was a reporter for a Vancouver newspaper, Wendy worked at the University of Washington, and Tony worked at the Yukon Travel department. Nancy hadn't had much experience as a group leader, and this high-energy group might have driven even an experienced leader insane.

Only a mile or so from the lodge the road was washed out so badly that no 4-wheel vehicle could cross. As we struggled across the gap, Nancy mentioned that no hunters could penetrate past this point in trucks, so game would be plentiful from here on. The evidence of game was everywhere, because the hard graveled surface of the Canol makes a perfect game trail and all the large animals use it. Tracks, and what the locals politely refer to as 'sign', of grizzly bear, moose, caribou, and wolf were everywhere. To these we added our own distinctive marks, fat-tyre tracks.

Low willows grow thickly along the sides of the road, a natural habitat for bears. Sam had told us, 'These are wild grizzlies, not park bears. They're not used to people, and they aren't nearly as fierce as people think they are. If they hear you coming mostly they'll just run away. But if you come around a corner fast and run into one, or scare a cub, you're in trouble.' Accordingly we held our pace to a very reasonable speed, and whistled and sang with enthusiasm to give Mr. or Ms. Bear time to amble off the trail.

We saw plenty of moose tracks, but no moose. It's not that they only come out at night, because it doesn't really get dark. As Nancy explained, 'Moose are experts

**The *n*the crossing of the Ekwi. With road and river constantly looping back over each other, there was never a dry—or warm—moment.**

at standing still when they don't want to be seen. We probably passed close by several standing near the road in the low brush, and while they saw us, we didn't see them.'

Following the watershed down a valley, we came on one of the old work camps left from the time when the road was built. The officers' quarters have been turned into a makeshift stable for the pack trains that use the road, and the walls are marked with many scribbled names and dates. In front is a line of trucks that were once parked in a neat row, but have been moved around by the action of the permafrost and the salvagers who retrieved the tyres and wheels long ago, before the road became impassable to vehicles. A few dozen barrels are stacked as they have been for forty years, and the unhealed scars of a shallow quarry which supplied the gravel road surface attests to the length of time it takes for the tundra to recover from the insult. On a cliff high above the camp a pair of golden eagles observed us from their nest, and the scrawny head of their chick peeped over the edge of the nest.

Descending to the first creek crossing we encountered another form of northern wildlife, one that seems in little danger of extinction. Between the mosquitoes and the blackflies (known Red Indian-style as 'no see-ums') Canada has 130 species of biting insects; some say the national bird is the mosquito. These creatures hardly qualify as insects.

At this first crossing some of us carefully took off our shoes and socks before wading across, the last time anyone took such precautions. With water blocking our route every mile or so, we got used to striding into the cold, hip-deep water in jeans and boots. Cold and wet feet are a fact of life in this country, and since everyone has them, it's no use complaining. After all, isn't adventure defined as discomfort that you brag about afterwards?

When lunch time came, we dropped our bikes in the middle of the road and sat down, not for a moment thinking that we would be in anyone's way. But as we sat eating lunch on the road we heard the unmistakable sound of a tiny engine, truly a surprise. Presently a tiny trail motorbike appeared, a Honda 70 loaded down with an inflatable rubber raft, a rifle, tent and sleeping bag, food, camera gear, and under all that, a rider who was as surprised at seeing us as we were to see him. He introduced himself as Archie Knill, and he told us that he had started his journey the previous summer from Norman Wells at the end of the Canol. Caught in August the year before by inclement weather, he had stored his bike at a hunting camp and flown out, returning nearly a year later to retrieve his bike and complete his trip. He told us of a harrowing river crossing the year before, when his raft had capsized and dumped all his gear and motorcycle. After fishing it all out, he had to dis-assemble and clean his motor on the bank before continuing.

Archie told us about what we would be facing the next day when we followed the Ekwi River. 'I had to cross it seven times', he reassured us, 'But you can carry your bikes, so you shouldn't have any trouble except the last one, where it's pretty deep.' We assured him that he had nothing that difficult ahead of him. Archie also gave us a couple of what we were beginning to realise were in everyone's repertoire here, the 'I've been chased by bears' story. Grizzlies are more numerous than people here, so people living in the area are bound to run across them once in a while or even more often. No-one who told such a story had actually been eaten by a bear, and in fact recorded instances of such behaviour on the part of bears are extremely rare in the NWT, but everyone had apparently escaped the Canadian version of JAWS by the merest of margins. It seems to be a tradition in the north to regale travellers with bear stories before letting them venture into bear territory.

Our first night's camp was at a tiny cabin Sam had built from the telephone poles that had once stood by the road but had fallen years before from the action of the permafrost. Other materials for the cabin had come from the remains of washed out bridges, since there were no trees of any kind in the valley. Before we could enter the cabin we had to remove the 'bear boards', nail studded, iron bound boards that were bolted over the door and window to keep out curious grizzlies. One corner of the cabin had been clawed by a bear seeking entry, and Sam had told us that it was because it had smelled the chain saw oil inside. 'They seem to love petroleum products', he said, 'they'll drink motor oil if they can find it.'

Sam had made a labourious trip to deliver a food supply and some firewood to the cabin a few days before, and a bush pilot had flown a cache out to our next camp. Accordingly, we ate very well with Nancy putting together excellent dinners, and breakfasts of 'bannock', a staple of the north. Bannock is flour, water, and salt, fried in oil and washed down with 'camp coffee', made by dumping grounds into boiling water and drinking the result. There are two schools of drinking such coffee. Some strain the grounds through teeth or moustache, while others chew them thoughtfully while expounding on what fun they are having.

The next day was as clear and warm as the one previous, and it seemed hard to believe that this country lies under ice and snow most of the year. As we followed the valley of the Ekwi the road deteriorated, until we found ourselves struggling down a canyon with sheer sides and no trace of the road. Ironically, in this otherwise trackless place, the track of Archie's Honda assured us that we were headed the right direction. Now we started river crossing in earnest. The slippery rocks and the deep, cold rushing water made it quite a chore to carry a bike loaded with touring gear across, but removing panniers and ferrying everything across in several loads would have taken far too much time considering how many times we would need to cross. Since the women couldn't lift their bikes high enough to keep gear out of the stream, at first they unloaded their bikes for stream crossings, but this took so long that we took up a routine in which each of the men first carried his bike across and then returned for one of the women's, not out of any displaced sense of chivalry, but for reasons of efficiency.

As we struggled down the canyon, a grizzly perhaps a quarter mile away on the other side of the valley ran into the brush and disappeared. High above on the barren ridge, a lone bull caribou profiled his magnificent antlers against the sky.

We found the road again after exiting the canyon, but this took some searching after we lost the Honda track on rocky ground. Forty years of erosion changes the lay of the land, so when we found the gravel surface, it seemed to be in an unlikely place. Later that day we came to a plain of river rocks that had cascaded out of a steep valley during a sudden thaw some years before. The mile-wide expanse of rock and gravel, barren of plant life, gave no indication of where the road had been, so we spread out in a line as we picked our individual ways across, looking for indications of travel or the place where the road resumed. It wasn't easy, and it took a considerable amount of hiking along the clearly defined edge of the gravel plain before we found the faint track.

It was late in the day before we covered the 35 miles to our next camp, but during the Arctic summer the sun is up nearly all the time. Finally we spotted the small landing strip and hunting outfitter's cabin where we hoped our food had been left by the bush pilot. Sure enough, next to the strip was our food packed in a padlocked steel barrel to keep the bears out, so we loaded our panniers with enough supplies for dinner and breakfast, leaving the rest to be retrieved later.

We spent the next day exploring, hiking, and fishing in the area, and we were

**Bear-proof cabin, a Northwest Territory waystation for travellers**

surprised to meet several more people. Although there aren't many in the region, those who are here concentrate their activities around what's left of the Canol. The first to run across our camp were a German couple, hiking on their way to Oldsquaw from Norman Wells. The news they brought us of a river too deep and wide for us to cross meant that we had gone as far as we could get without a raft, so we cancelled our plan to strike farther up the road. Experienced hikers in this area, they also regaled us with a few of own their narrow 'bear-escape' stories.

That evening the forest stillness was broken by the sound of an aircraft engine as a helicopter followed the road past our camp. The pilot circled and settled in for a landing a few hundred feet from us. The visit was strictly social, and typical of this sparsely populated area, the pilot had heard of Nancy Eagleson and Sam Miller, so he and Nancy filled each other in on the local news and we gave the pilot and his two passengers coffee. The pilot asked if some of us would like a quick flight, and we jumped at the chance. An aerial touring service, in the middle of nowhere!

Our thrilling ride lasted only a few minutes, but covered more territory than we could have seen in a week on bicycles, as we swooped over rugged peaks whose heights are rarely if ever seen by humans. Then suddenly we were back on the ground saying our goodbyes. In half an hour the helicopter would be at Oldsquaw, two cycling days away.

Without a raft there was no possibility of our continuing up the Canol, because this would have required crossing the increasingly deep and swift Ekwi River where the German couple told us they had been forced to swim while toting their gear on a makeshift float. The next day when we turned back on our path for the return trip we found the going much easier because we knew what to expect. Still, it took until late in the day to reach our first camp site at Caribou Pass some 35 miles away.

As we stopped for lunch next to the river, we were surprised by the sight of a bull caribou running unsteadily down the middle of the stream. A large bloody wound on his neck showed that he had only moments before escaped a hungry predator, probably a wolf. We theorised that the long-legged animal had eluded pursuit by running down the stream, which would have been more difficult for a smaller wolf.

We spent another day exploring the Caribou Pass area, and we had a few anxious moments when Nancy and Tony were long overdue on a hike. It turned out that they had encountered a bear, and had gone a much longer route than originally planned in order to avoid him. Because there are so many uncomfortable reasons for overdue hikers in this country, those of us left in camp grew increasingly worried as the two failed to show. Al got on his bike and started slowly down the road in the direction where we expected them to come from. To our vast relief, they showed up, several hours late, and coming from an unexpected direction due to their detour. But now Al was missing, and he didn't know that the two had returned on a different route!

If we were worried about two together, we were now even more worried about one alone and overdue, searching for people who were no longer out there. Although the sun doesn't really set, as it sinks behind the hills and the air cools, the bears who escape the midday heat by sleeping in the willows along the stream become more active. And Al was travelling alone, next to the stream. Our imaginations provided us with a host of tragic endings to our tour.

Finally, I couldn't stand it any longer, and together with Tony I started after Al. We hadn't gone half a mile when we saw the sweetest possible sight, Al's red and white striped shirt moving toward us in the darkening distance. More than any other incident of the tour, this reminded us that whatever our differences, we were all in this together. What started out as a loose group became a team at this point.

With everyone accounted for we could finally relax. Nancy and Tony regaled us with the most recent bear story, which now seemed to be the most amusing of all we had heard, just because it was so close to us.

Although we looked constantly for bears from that point on, we hoped we wouldn't see any, and we didn't. But there was plenty of other wildlife in the area. From our camp we could see Dall sheep on the high ridges, and tracks in our camp indicated that a parade of fauna had passed in the night only a few yards from where we were sleeping, including moose, wolf, and wolverine.

The clear weather held until our last day of riding, when skies turned leaden and a cold wind whistled down the valley. Summer rainfall here doesn't amount to much, but summer doesn't amount to much either, and winter can drop in at any time. Nancy told us that the year before it had snowed heavily in the middle of August; this was the storm that had forced Archie Knill to abandon his Honda for nearly a year. Accordingly, we didn't waste any time getting back to Oldsquaw. There is an amazing difference between wet feet on a warm day and wet feet on a cold day. The sauna at the lodge was a magnet.

By late afternoon we were all back at the lodge, clean, warm, well fed, beers in hand, and ready to match bear stories with any local citizen. The next day we would begin the three-day trip back to our civilised haunts with a new respect for our bikes and ourselves.

**Fisher Mountain Bikes Competition**

# Mountain Bike Anatomy

Any attempt to generalise on the set up and equipment of a 'typical' mountain bike is certain to run afoul of the many custom and unusual treatments used to tailor bikes to certain riders or local conditions. Regional differences and influences play a major part in design among those on the experimental end of the sport.

Of course, most riders will not be on custom equipment. However, mass-produced bikes are profoundly influenced by custom designers and builders. The starting point for mass-produced mountain bikes was Tom Ritchey's frame production in 1979, the first to be offered commercially. Because the field was so new, the mass-marketers did their best to copy something that was already proven successful. The result is that even though other builders were active at the same time, Ritchey's design influence was considerable during the beginning of the movement.

For this reason and because the first companies importing Japanese mountain bikes were based in California, the typical mass-produced mountain bike has been dubbed the 'California Style' by those in other parts of the United States who care to make such judgements. This is a little unfair to the California designers other than Ritchey who have their own definite ideas, and whose bikes don't show that much Ritchey influence. While it might be stretching the point to suggest that builders go out of their way to avoid the California influence, several other regions where mountain biking is strong have come up with their own styles that represent major departures from the geometry and features most riders associate with mountain bikes or the California Style.

The starting point for the modern mountain bike design was the customized cantilever-frame bike from the thirties. Having no backlog of theory on the subject of balloon-tyre bikes, the first Northern California builders merely duplicated the geometry of the most popular of the old frames, the Schwinn Excelsior X. This is a long-wheelbase bike, about 44 inches depending on how severely the fork had been pounded, with 'slack' geometry. Head tube is about 68 degrees and seat is 70. The chain stays are long at 18.5 inches.

Road-frame builders are used to working with steeper angles, and just as soon as mountain bikes appeared on the market, this faction began contributing designs with shorter wheelbases and steeper angles. Although it might seem like heresy, as soon as slack-angled mountain bikes became the rage, some frame designers began building bikes with head angles as steep as 74 degrees, which is considered steep even on a road bike. Chain stays were shortened to the minimum possible length for better climbing.

In bike design, everything is a trade-off. A bike designed for extreme lightness gives up something in strength, and vice versa. Attempts to maximise steering response by steepening the steering angle will result in a decrease in high-speed stability. Shortening the chain stay for better climbing traction gives up high-speed stability also, since this shortens the wheelbase, and changes the front wheel to back wheel weight ratio.

Customary bicycle wisdom says that the longer the wheelbase, the more comfortable the ride; this effect is commonly attributed to the fact that a longer piece of metal will have more overall spring, but there is another factor at work. Some frame builders claim that nearly any frame is so stiff in the vertical plane that differences are imperceptible to the rider, but the shorter the wheelbase, the more of an angular rotation the frame will go through when it encounters an irregularity in the road surface, which translates to more bike movement under the rider. The trade-off on wheelbase for mountain bikes is that the shorter the bike, the more overall ground clearance the bike will have at the bottom bracket. Each designer decides for himself what he is willing to give up in one area to improve performance in another.

Bicycle design is as much voodoo as it is science. Unlike road cycles, mountain bikes do not have a history of many decades of experiments and results, and they have evolved not so much on the drawing board as in practice. Even the expert builder can only generalize about a bike's performance during the design stage; the proof of whatever theory is being applied comes when he swings the leg over for the first time. Mountain bike performance is not as easily measured as road bike performance, because the most severe tests for mountain bikes and riders do not take place on a banked track or other controlled location. Also, since mountain bikes are used for such a wide range of activities in a complete spectrum of terrains, the subject lends itself to endless modification and tinkering.

What is the best design? It depends on whom you are asking and where you plan to ride. As I mentioned, there are regional schools of thought. As distinct as the California style is what might be called the 'Seattle' style which favours short wheelbase, high bottom bracket, and different size wheels. Cannondale and Raleigh of America have both brought out bikes along these lines, featuring a 24-inch rear wheel and a

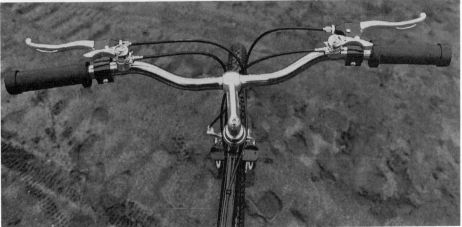

**Top: One-piece bullmoose pattern. Bottom: two-piece**

bottom bracket somewhat higher than the 12 or so inches of more conservative designs. The reason given for the Seattle influence is that riders in the Northwest have a vast network of trails through logging country available to ride. With numerous small logs to ride over, the Northwest riders developed a bike whose design is similar to that of a bike made for Observed Trials, with a high bottom bracket and short wheelbase.

The last few years have seen an explosion of materials and joining techniques introduced to bicycle technology, an extension of the uses of materials originally developed for space exploration and aviation. As such an experimental area, mountain bikes seem to inspire builders to try new combinations. A number of builders use aluminium oversize tubing, which was originally made popular for road bicycles by Gary Klein. Aluminium bicycles have certain advantages for lightness and stiffness over steel bikes, and they are resistant to corrosion. Although the heli-arc welding is simple, aluminium bikes can be tricky to make because the heat-treating process demands considerable care to prevent the frame from becoming warped. Because aluminium is less springy than steel and more subject to metal fatigue, it is not popular as material for forks. By using a different tube-joining technology, such as glue joints, builders can use springier alloys of aluminium alloys that can't be welded. This permits the use of smaller diameter tubing for a frame that isn't as stiff as one made from oversize tubing. Composite tubing will be a major factor in the bicycle market in years to come in combinations of aluminium or steel with carbon or boron fibre.

For some designers, ultimate stiffness is not the goal. As I mentioned, there is debate from both sides of the issue on whether and how the rider is affected by the stiffness of the frame tubing and how much stiffness is a desirable characteristic of a mountain bike. Proponents of steel tubing point out that the diameter of bike tubing has been developed over a considerable length of time for maximum comfort. Steel also has a few advantages over aluminium in wear characteristics.

Since the characteristics of aluminium and steel are good for different types of performance, why not use both in different parts of the bike? In smaller diameters of tubing, steel gains the weight advantage because small diameter aluminium tubes must be made with much thicker walls to give comparable performance. Because of the clearance problems associated with the use of fat tyres, mountain bike design is easier if the chain stays are made of small diameter tubing. Several designers are now building composite frames using an aluminium main triangle and steel stays. Steel stays also allow the builder to use a steel drop-out, which is tougher than an aluminium drop-out.

Chain stay clearance is one of the more complicated aspects of mountain bike design. Originally, bottom bracket spindles for 10-speeds were made to a length that assumed that the bike used a narrow tyre. The crank had to extend far enough from the frame so it would clear the tyre and the chain stay. The introduction of multiple gear mountain bikes complicated the problem, because the wider tyre would snag on the chain. The wider tyre made it necessary to push the chain line out a little bit. This was done by increasing the standard rear axle length from 120 mm (old 5-speed standard) or 126 mm (6-speed standard) to 130 mm, which has become the standard for mountain bikes. The bottom bracket spindle was lengthened accordingly. As an example of how one thing affects another, the longer spindle in turn put new demands on front derailleurs, since nothing designed strictly for 10-speeds would push the chain far enough out from the seat tube to put it on the outer gear.

This leads into the subject of mountain bike components. In the beginning of the movement builders used a hodge-podge of 10-speed parts, motorcycle parts, tandem parts, and components designed for BMX, along with a frame that might be forty years old. After mountain bikes became respectable enough for the major manufacturers to see a market in them, the two major Japanese component manufacturers, Shimano and Suntour, brought out product lines for them. These two giants dominate the market, because home mechanics are unlikely to be turning out derailleurs and shift levers in the garage; still, the individual entrepreneur retains an important place in the continuing development of mountain bikes.

Items such as seat posts, handlebars, and brake sets are within the capabilities of most adept machinists, and much of the progress in these areas has been made by riders who were frustrated with the available components.

**Cannondale's mid-range SM500. Made from oversize aluminium tubing, a material that is light and corrosion-free**

Handlebars in particular have received quite a bit of attention. This is due to two reasons; first, handlebar position affects the rider position a great deal, and second, handlebars are the next obvious item for the frame builder to make, since they are made of the same material.

Handlebars have evolved in several ways. Joe Breeze's first bikes used motorcycle handlebars and a conventional stem. Tom Ritchey introduced the first trend in mountain bike handlebars with the one-piece triangulated version. The obvious problem with these is that there is no adjustment possible. Manufacturers responded by producing a variety of different bends, widths, and amounts of rise in their handlebars, but the inherent limitations of this design have inspired designers to move away from it.

The most obvious departure from the triangulated handlebar is the use of drop bars like those used on road bikes. There are a number of proponents of this style, and regardless of the fact that they are in the minority, it's hard to argue with success. Jacquie Phelan and Charlie Cunningham both rode drop bars to national mountain bike championships, and a number of other top racers have sworn by them. Drop bars are especially popular in Crested Butte, where the number of mountain bikes per capita is probably the highest in the world.

Most riders using drop handlebars modify them slightly from the original bend by spreading the bar ends. There is a limit to how much a set of aluminium bars can isbe reshaped, and in order to get an even wider spread, American designers started making their own designs from steel tubing. One of the more intriguing versions is very similar to the racing handlebars used at the turn of the century, about half-way between a drop bar and a flat handlebar. By using drop handlebars, designers limit the use of shifters and brake levers designed for flat bars. One choice is a bar-end shifter, but some riders still use a thumb-shifter mounted next to a standard road brake lever.

The trend away from the one-piece triangulated handlebar has led to the two-piece flat handlebar. Manufacturers have introduced new stems that give the necessary rise, and the handlebar itself is little more than a piece of slightly bent tubing. By adjusting the stem height or trying several different bends, the rider can customise his position more completely than he can with the one-piece type.

The handlebar possibilities are a long way from exhausted. Among the unusual designs is a set of flat handlebars with right-angle extensions, very similar to the handlebars used on high-tech time-trial bicycles. Another designer has put together a set of drop bars with a quick-release stem for height adjustment.

The seat post quick-release is standard on most mountain bikes. The original reason for this component is so the rider could raise and lower the saddle easily to deal with changing conditions; in general it is raised for climbing so the rider can get full leg extension and stay in the saddle to control traction, and lowered for control on descents. But riders found that it took time and a dismount to make the adjustment, and as they strove for more efficiency during races, they didn't want to lose even these few seconds. Also, when the rider wanted to raise his saddle, he had to be careful to get it back to optimum height and keep it aligned with the frame, and this took more time. The seat post quick-release was in danger of becoming an anachronism.

A number of designers addressed this problem with various spring devices, but it was left to mountain bike pioneer Joe Breeze to come up with the idea that made the seat post quick-release efficient. The patented device, called the Hite-Rite, is now standard on many of the more expensive mountain bikes; essentially it is a spring and two clamps that return the saddle to a pre-set height and keep it aligned with the frame.

## Toe Clip or Not Toe Clip
### (that's the question)

For the clunker riders of Northern California the toe clip was symbolic of everything they were trying to get away from. The pedals designed for BMX worked quite well without toe clips and straps, and besides, you needed to get a foot off the pedal to control slides on gonzo downhills.

In order to get more grip from a pedal without toe clips, manufacturers designed a class of pedals affectionately known as 'bear traps', which replaced the 'rat trap' BMX pedals. The name bear trap comes from the round or oval pedal cage with a serrated edge. My observation is that you don't slip off these pedals for two reasons; first, because they have a good grip, and second because the teeth would be certain to damage your leg.

As racing got more intense, those interested in top performance had to allow that the rider is more efficient if his feet are firmly attached to the pedals. They also observed that on very rough descents, toe clips kept the rider from slipping off the pedals if he had enough confidence in his riding to use them. Mountain bike races are generally won on the climbs rather than the descents, so riders didn't mind sacrificing some gonzo capability.

One trick of riding with toe clips and straps is getting back into them after a dismount, which can be difficult on a steep climb. Several manufacturers have brought out a small metal tab for the edge of the pedal that catches the shoe sole and lines up the pedal for a quick step-in.

# Buying a Mountain Bike

Now and then (far too often) I am asked by someone who is considering purchasing a bike, 'What is the best mountain bike?' What an innocent-sounding, but far-reaching question! It is impossible to answer because there are so many decisions that go into the purchase of a bicycle (any bicycle, not just a mountain bike).

Often my questioner will be armed with the latest collection of bicycle reviews from a cycling publication, which only adds to my burden of explanation. Speaking as someone who has been forced to write 'bike reviews', I believe that such articles are a waste of good paper. (Save a tree; shoot a bike reviewer!) Bike reviews are designed not so much to inform the reader as they are designed to sell advertising and magazines. Ad salespersons find it much easier to push a full page of colour advertising on a company if the magazine contains a glowing review of the product. For this reason, few bikes are found to be entirely wanting, and negative comments are often edited, eliminated, or disinfected. Also, by promising the full scoop on the latest bikes in red letters on the cover of the issue, the publisher hopes that prospective bike purchasers will pick up the magazine and take it home before they find out that the review contains little information that the reader couldn't find out by visiting a bike shop where the product is sold.

Any perusal of a collection of bike reviews will show that they are largely the same review with only the names and the specifications changed; for example, steering is often described as 'nimble', 'responsive', or some other meaningless adjective. Bicycle performance defies numerical analysis, and reviews are often nothing more than a subjective analysis of the way a test bike compares with the reviewer's personal machine.

There is the question of how much the purchaser has to spend. Given the unlimited choice, I might settle for a hand-crafted, custom-measured frameset made of the most exotic aerospace tubing known to man, equipped with gold-plated componentry with my initials engraved in every flat surface. Since I have not been given the unlimited choice, I have settled for a very nice semi-custom frameset from a well-known builder, a bike that satisfies my personal needs.

What's so different about bikes costing £200 and bikes that cost £1,000? If you need to ask this question, you haven't ridden a really nice custom bike to compare performance with that of a relatively inexpensive mass-produced one. Custom or really nice bikes really are more fun to ride, although most riders will not be able to define the difference in performance other than saying that the bike feels faster, and of course expensive bikes are usually more durable over the extremely long run. Most people do not ride a bicycle near enough to its performance limits to notice any difference, and most people who get cheap bikes either don't ride them or eventually get something nicer. (For people who don't intend to ride a bike but need to purchase one for image reasons, of course it makes sense to get the cheapest possible machinery.) So most people can be and are satisfied with ordinary cycling equipment. If on the other hand a bicycle is important to you for any reason, it makes sense to get a nice one to start with. Why delay the inevitable?

Aside from price, there are several other major factors to consider when purchasing a mountain bike. What will it be used for? Touring? Racing? Single-day excursions? Grocery shopping? While the same bike may be capable of satisfying all these demands, if the purchaser intends to concentrate on a single type of riding (racing especially), this may colour the decision.

Then we get to the question of sizing. Depending on whose advice you read, the mountain bike frame should be from 1 to 3 inches smaller than a road bike for the same rider. I'm glad we narrowed that down.

There is one problem with all the expert opinions on frame sizing. Human bodies come in several billion unique configurations, while bicycles come in somewhat less variety of frame dimensions and geometry, something like three or four at the average bike shop. Each of us must drag his or her uniquely designed carcass down to the bike shop and select from less than half a dozen sizes and designs. There is only one test for size that works, and that is to ride a selection of bikes and choose the most comfortable. If in the process of testing bikes for fit, you can't tell the difference in performance between a cheap bike and an expensive bike, by all means buy the cheap one.

Frame size is always given as the measure of seat tube length, but aside from this variable, reach is a big factor in comfort. Reach is not necessarily related to leg length, since a rider with short legs might have a long torso or long arms. But bikes are designed for an average rider who does not exist except statistically (a more cynical view is that most mass-produced mountain bikes are designed around the personal dimensions of the frame builders who first introduced custom versions to the market). Reach is not only a matter of the distance from the saddle to the handlebars, it is also a matter of handlebar width and the relative level of the bars compared to the saddle. The wider the bars, the farther forward the rider leans. Once again, there are as many expert opinions on how much reach is necessary as there are experts, and each rider should make his or her own 'expert' judgement. Proper reach will distribute the weight comfortably, and will not cause the rider to lean so far forward that the position becomes uncomfortable on a long ride.

Since the mountain biker is usually on a smaller frame than the road biker, the seat post extends further from the frame on a mountain bike. This means that the relationship between the saddle height and the height of the top of the steering tube is different than on a road bike; on a mountain bike the saddle is an inch or more higher in relation to the top of the head tube. What this is getting around to is that the mountain biker doesn't need a stem that drops the handlebars, he needs one that raises them. The height of the bars isn't chiselled in stone. They should be adjusted for a height and reach that is comfortable. (Don't let a salesperson tell you what is comfortable. Decide for yourself.)

Now consider reach. Aren't the handlebars too wide? Of course they are if they are like 90 per cent of the handlebars out there, especially if the rider has a short reach; this includes most women. The theory is that it's easier to make handlebars shorter than it is to make them longer. If they are too wide, don't be afraid to cut them down. If you want to cut the bars down, start by moving the controls, the shifters and the brake levers, toward the middle and see how the position feels before getting out the hack-saw. It's a good idea to take off small amounts several times rather than to take off too much with a big cut. A small difference in handlebar width can make a major difference in the way they feel.

I once accompanied Tom Ritchey on a trip to Japan, where someone showed him one of his early mountain bikes that had been brought over there a couple of years before. The handlebars were incredibly wide, and Tom asked, 'Why didn't you cut them down?' The startled owner replied that that was how wide he thought they should be. Tom had assumed that every owner would trim them to appropriate size. Perhaps this set of handlebars or others like them influenced Japanese handlebar design; I read a review of a mountain bike in a mainstream magazine, and the reviewer's comments included the statement that '. . . at about 33 inches, the handlebars were somewhat wide . . . .' I'll say they were! I'm a 6-footer with long arms, and the bars on my bike are around 24 inches wide.

Mountain bikes have higher bottom brackets than road bikes to make it easier for riders to clear rocks, logs, or whatever other obstacles they encounter. This is the reason frame sizes for mountain bikers are smaller than for road cyclists; it is inconvenient to raise the top tube a similar amount, because this would make it hard for the rider to straddle the frame and stand on the ground. A mountain bike will have a shorter seat tube to keep the top tube at the same height. To compensate for the shorter seat tube, a mountain bike rider extends the seat post further from the frame than the road cyclist does. In fact, the trend toward mountain bikes has created a new standard length for seat posts longer than the standard length for road bikes.

# Rims, Knobbies and Slicks

It is likely that the modern mountain bike movement would not exist if riders still had to contend with the wheels that originally got things rolling. The original Northern California clunkers were usually built with drum brake hubs, and used the heaviest tyres and steel rims on the market. The result was a pair of wheels that only a purist could love.

Rims of choice were either the Schwinn S-2 in the 2.125-inch width or any 26 × 1.75-inch rim. The advantage to the 1.75-inch rim was that it was narrower and lighter, but it wasn't a box-section like the S-2, so it wasn't as strong. The S-2 might be strong, but it was as heavy as an anchor (as was the drum brake hub and the tyre).

Garage mechanics can turn out bike frames, but when it comes to components they are at the mercy of the manufacturers. It's hard to turn out aluminium rims in the back yard. When Joe Breeze built the first modern chrome-moly clunkers he saved considerable weight by using cantilever brakes rather than drums. The reason drum brakes had caught on in the first place is that using them was the easiest way to convert a coaster-brake bike to a multi-speed. Some clunker riders used cantilever brakes on the front wheels of their converted clunkers because there were a few old pairs of Schwinn cantilever brakes around which would clamp onto the flat fork blade, but using cantilevers on the rear wheel of an old frame had problems. Because the seat tube on an old cantilever frame is so short and because riders used the longest cranks they could find for climbing leverage, the rider's heel would hit the projecting cantilever in the rear. Also, the use of rim brakes on steel rims did not give riders the stopping power it took to ride Repack on a misty morning.

Calliper brakes were considered unusable because the length of the arms necessary to wrap around the fat tyre contributed so much flex and stretching to the brake system. Under wet conditions having calliper brakes on a clunker was like having no brakes. So the average clunker owner's wheels were built on drum brakes scrounged from some obscure source. In fact, on occasion riders had to go to some lengths to obtain these components, whose use at the time was confined to some tandems. One drum brake that was available in good supply was a front hub originally made for a line of 20-inch bikes; the problem was that it was drilled for 28 spokes. Riders patiently re-drilled them, creating some interesting spoking patterns in the process.

By dispensing with the drum-brake hub Breeze had saved several pounds on the wheels. (It is worth noting that other off-road designers had also used cantilever brakes, which are popular on cyclo-cross bikes because they don't catch as much mud as calliper brakes. In 1953 John Finley Scott's 'Woodsy Bike', which in all major respects resembled a modern mountain bike, had been equipped with cantilever brakes.) As the number of custom mountain bikes in California grew to several dozen, the owners began praying that a rim manufacturer would do something about their heavy steel wheels.

Customary bicycle wisdom as applied to road bikes is that 'An ounce on the rim equals a pound on the bike.' In other words, because the rim and tyre are rotating weight, a saving in this area increases performance as much as taking a much larger amount of weight off the bike as a whole. If taking an ounce off the rim is equivalent to taking a pound off the rest of the bike, the improvement in performance when several Japanese manufacturers introduced aluminium 26-inch rims that saved two pounds from the S-2 rims was a quantum leap. A short time later, 'gumwall' 26 × 2.125-inch tyres came on the market, which were a pound each lighter than the old Uniroyal knobbies that were the tyre of choice (or perhaps the absence of choice) for clunker riders. A total saving of six pounds, all on the rim, took mountain bike performance from the stone age to the mainstream. Cyclists whose only experience with balloon-tyre bikes had been on the heavy wheels could not believe how fast and agile the bikes had become. As much as the introduction of chrome-moly framesets got things started, the availability of aluminium alloy rims and light tyres made mountain bikes what they are today.

The wheel revolution was not quite over. Hubs were the next component to be modified for mountain bike use. Frame builders found that the wider tyre created problems with the chain line and chain stay clearance. When the chain was on the small inner chainring on a triple front set up and on the inner cog on the cluster, the knobs on the side of the tyre could actually catch the chain and drag it between the tyre and the chain stay. The problem was compounded by the fact that the bike was often bouncing around and the chain was somewhat slack because the derailleur was close to its capacity for taking up chain.

The solution was to widen the rear hub and move the cluster further away from the centreline. Standard 5-speed rear hub width is 120 mm between the drop-outs. When 6-speed clusters became popular, 6-speed spacing became 125 or 126 mm. For mountain bikes the standard for rear spacing became 130 mm. The slightly wider hub gives the wheel more strength side-to-side and reduces the amount of 'dish' or asymmetry made necessary by the presence of the cluster.

(Because the components of a bicycle operate as a system, a change in one dimension can force changes in another. In order to keep the chain line straight, builders increased the length of the bottom bracket spindle; this was done also to provide more clearance for the inner chainring from the chain stay, since the chain stay was also pushed out from the centreline by the wider tyre. With the chainrings now farther away from the seat tube, front derailleurs had to be redesigned to reach out farther. Thus, the use of the wider tyre brought about new standards for the rear hub, the front derailleur, and the bottom bracket spindle.)

Now that mountain bikes have taken over a major share of the bicycle market, there is a bewildering multitude of rims and tyres available. Rims are beginning to fall into the categories of narrow and narrower, while tyres are divided into three broad categories: off-road, mixed-use, and street. As a general rule the off-road tyre will have a very rough and knobby tread pattern, the mixed-use tyre will have some tread along with a raised centre strip for fast rolling when the bike is on a hard surface and travelling in a straight line, and the street tyre will have a smooth tread or none at all.

Because the fat tyre is not too fussy about the size of rim it inhabits it can be fitted onto rims from 1.5 to over 2 inches wide. Tyres themselves vary in width from 1.5 to 2.2 inches; in general the narrower tyres give up a little durability in order to gain a little speed.

Mountain bike tyres and wheels, which were once the heaviest that could be found, are evolving back toward their skinnier cousins as riders search for the maximum performance value versus reasonable durability. With the use of a Kevlar bead, manufacturers have reduced the weight of a racing fat tyre to under 600 grams. An extra benefit of using the Kevlar bead is that the tyre folds up easily enough to be carried under the saddle. By using a 1.75-inch (aluminium alloy) rim instead of a 2.125-inch, the rider can save about 200 grams; because most tyres will fit the 1.75-inch and because the narrower rim is still considerably stronger than a road rim, most riders opt for 1.75-inch and the 2.125-inch rim is increasingly rare. The use of a 1.5-inch rim can save another 100 grams, but the widest tyres may be difficult to mount. Also, reducing the rim width reduces the size of the air chamber that provides the cushioning effect on rough ground.

It is well known and widely reported that the majority of 'mountain bikes' don't see much if any service on dirt roads. Recognising this, manufacturers have introduced for mountain bikes the bald tyre, a concept that at first defies conventional tyre logic, but which has proven itself at the highest level of professional road racing. Treadless tyres corner amazingly well, even under wet conditions, as demonstrated by several tests by reasonably sceptical test crews. Because fat tyres are now being designed for pressures of up to 6 atmospheres, the rolling resistance has been reduced considerably for street use. Many sets of wheels made for mountain bikes are lighter than the wheels on lower priced 10-speeds and 'middleweight' bicycles.

I have even seen a set of the slick tyres used on the Pearl Pass ride in Colorado,

**Fattrax 202, a lightweight knobby competition tyre weighing just 699 grams**

and the rider claimed his traction, even on loose dirt, was as good as any. The major drawback of slick tyres is the fact that their durability is reduced by the short distance between the casing and the ground. On a knobby tyre any foreign object that gets embedded in the rubber is usually stuck into one of the 'knobs', with perhaps half an inch of rubber to penetrate before it enters the casing. Without this protection the slick tyre is more vulnerable, especially in city use where broken glass and scraps of metal are more common than in the mountains.

Having mentioned inflation pressures of up to 6 atmospheres, I should point out that this is an extreme value. For years tyres came with this inscription on the side-wall: 'Inflate to 30-40 psi.' Since mountain bikers have never taken the manufacturer's word for anything, some enterprising type no doubt set out to find how much pressure would blow the tyre off the rim. The answer, it turned out, was a lot. For street riding high pressure reduces rolling resistance to values approximating those of middleweight tyres.

Several years ago on a trip to Japan I sat in on a design session with Tom Ritchey and a group of Japanese tyre manufacturers whom he was contracting to make his tyres. Tom mentioned that he would like the side-wall stamped 'Inflate to 80 psi', and the tyre makers blanched. It was not possible, they said, think of the liability problems. Tom casually informed them that he and everyone else had been inflating tyres to these pressures for years with no problems.

Tyre design has made an interesting revolution since the days when the Uniroyal was the only tyre worth riding. This heavy tyre had a knobby tread, but the cross-section of the tyre was decidedly square. Riders asked for, and got from the manufacturers, tyres with a round cross-section and wider spacing on the knobs. As the American designers refined their ideas about traction, they came up with designs that made the knobs on the side of the tyre taller than the ones in the middle in order to give the tyre more bite when it was leaned over into a corner. The result is that the cross-section of some modern tyres is once again square.

Off the road, a harder tyre gives a rougher ride and reduces climbing traction. At the other extreme, the softer the tyre the greater the rolling resistance and the greater the possibility of a rim-pinch puncture, the dreaded 'snake-bite'. For most riders the pressure used is 35-40 psi, a reasonable compromise. Observed Trials riders use very low pressure because they are not worried about durability and rolling resistance as much as they are concerned with traction.

Although there have been a few attempts to reinvent the mountain bike wheel by building with different lacings such as radial for the front wheel and a half-radial on the rear, the vast majority of riders and wheel-builders use the four-cross spoking pattern that has been the standard ever since early clunker riders discovered that a four-cross 26-inch wheel could be built with 270 mm spokes and nearly any combination of rim and hub.

Because saving weight on the rim improves bicycle performance, mountain bikers have come up with a few tricks. Electrical tape or packing tape on the rim instead of a rubber rim strip saves an ounce. Aluminium alloy nipples instead of brass can save a little over an ounce. The trade-off is that it is easier to break an aluminium spoke nipple if it becomes scored during the building process. Butted spokes save another ounce over straight-gauge, and moving up in spoke gauge can save weight, although spokes smaller than 15/16 butted might be a little suspect. Radial spoking saves even more weight, and proponents of this pattern insist that it is the strongest for a non-drive wheel, but as I mentioned, this pattern has not taken over the fat-tyre world. Manufacturers have developed lighter tubes along with lighter tyres, and some fanatical weight-savers will wrestle an undersized 24-inch tube into a 26-inch tyre.

# The
# Brake
# Debate

One of the most common impressions mountain bikes make on those trying them for the first time is that they have astonishing braking. Part of this feeling is the result of the increased grip the larger tyre has on the road, but in general it is true mountain bikes are equipped with brakes that are a step up from the braking systems on road bikes.

There is no 'best brake' for all conditions. Choice of brakes may vary depending on the rider's bicycle, riding style, and available terrain. There are several trade-offs between roller-cams, cantilevers, and drum brakes which can affect the choice, and each rider should consider the strengths and weaknesses of these designs in selecting a system.

Clunker riders abandoned their drum brakes for frame-mounted cantilevers as soon as frames became available with the welded-on pivots. This was because drum brakes had not proved any more effective and were heavier; in addition, drums had to be carefully adjusted for proper operation, and the extra cable attachments and brake arm attachments at the hub made wheel changes more complicated. The drum brakes the clunker riders were using were certainly not designed for off-road abuse and their durability was suspect; a common problem for riders on Repack was fading of hot drum brakes.

The dry California climate is well suited for rim brakes on mountain bikes, but it would be a disservice to suggest that drum brakes have no place any more on mountain bikes. In some climates where the roads are extremely muddy for long periods of time, rim brakes can clog with mud, and the constant scouring of muddy brake pads wears them out quickly. Also, drum brakes are not affected at all by bent rims.

In the past few years several new mountain bike brake designs have appeared, notably

**Cantilever brake**

the 'roller-cam', which, like the popular cantilever brake, requires a set of welded-on pivots, although the pivots are in a different location from the cantilever's, and the 'U-brake', which uses the same pivots as the roller-cam. The primary advantages of welded-on brakes are that (1) they are lighter than drums, (2) they can't vibrate loose, and (3) they provide more stopping power, especially to a wide wheel with a large tyre, than a traditional calliper brake because the arms are shorter and have less flex. These advantages are enough that virtually every off-road bike now sold uses welded-on brakes, either cantilever or roller-cam, with drum brakes and calliper brakes running far behind in popularity.

For perfect efficiency the ideal brake cable system should have no cable stretch or housing compression. Nothing is perfect, and as the cables stretch slightly and the cable housing compresses, efficiency is lost. On some bikes a short length of housing leads the rear brake cable to a set of cable stops on the frame and the bare brake cable runs between the cable stops. On other bikes the full length housing is routed through guides with no cable stops on the frame, which gives less efficient braking. Full length housing is usually a light gauge so it will fit through the standard cable guides found on less expensive bikes. The lighter gauge cable stretches more than the heavy-duty motorcycle cable used on the best custom bikes. Cable stops on the frame make for more efficient braking because they do not have any appreciable compression when the brake cable is pulled, and the bare cable run replaces a length of cable housing that would otherwise compress.

Because cantilever brake pivots are positioned between the rim and the axle, the stays or fork blades on which they are mounted can spread slightly when they are applied, adding springiness to the braking feel. Since cantilevers are mounted slightly

**Roller-cam brake**

farther away from the stay than roller-cams or U-brakes, they tend to twist the stay a little more when they are applied, once again adding springiness.

Roller-cam (U-brake) pivots are mounted outside the radius of the rim, closer to the cross-brace on the rear stays or the fork crown in front, so although the greater mechanical advantage puts increased forces on the frame, the forces are applied to a stronger part of the frame. The roller-cam brake provides a more solid feel than cantilevers or the U-brake, which is either good or bad depending on the rider's point of view. Some riders prefer the mushier cantilever feel, which they say allows them to fine-tune the braking; roller-cam adherents swear by the undeniable rim-gripping power of a well-adjusted set of these brakes. Still a third school of thought has a cantilever front and roller-cam or U-brake rear. This is an outgrowth of the observation that the stretching of the brake cable and the compression of the housing contribute some of the loss of efficiency in the braking system. Because the front cable is shorter it gives the front cantilever a more solid feel. The roller-cam will lock the wheel more easily than the cantilever because of its power-peak design, and some riders prefer a cantilever in front because it has less of a 'hair trigger'.

By contrast to roller-cam or U-brakes, cantilevers protrude from the frame, and can catch on panniers, clothing, or even flesh. A frayed yoke-cable end on the left side of a Mafac rear brake can leave the Mark of Zorro on the thigh when the rider is pushing the bike. (When Shimano introduced their Deore cantilever brake, they put the bare end of the yoke cable on the right side of the rear brake. Good thinking.) Cantilevers are also more vulnerable to being broken off than roller-cams, not only because the arm protrudes to the side of the frame, but also because the pivot is a smaller diameter and holds the brake arm farther off the stay or fork blade.

One problem with cantilevers appears when the pads are severely worn. Because of the location of the pivot, the pad strikes the rim at a progressively lower point as it wears down, and eventually, can dive under the rim. Theoretically this could catch a spoke and air-mail the rider, but in practise all that occurs is an absence of braking. As a roller-cam or U-brake pad wears, it strikes the rim higher, which leads to less dramatic problems; in the roller-cam the brake may lose efficiency because the cam adjustment changes, or if the pads encounter the tyre they can wear out the side-wall.

A disadvantage to roller-cams appears when they are mounted under the chain stays and the rider encounters deep and sticky mud. Perhaps because these brakes were developed in a part of California where mud is not an ongoing problem, they are at their best when used under relatively dry conditions. The small pulleys and cam plate are vulnerable to clogging by slime build-up, and this problem has spurred several manufacturers to develop add-on cloth covers for this vital area.

## Mechanical Advantage

The basic measure of a bicycle brake's mechanical performance (as opposed to the coefficient of friction of the brake pad) is how much pressure is put on the rim, that is, the mechanical advantage of the system. Mechanical advantage has two elements: the design of the system, and the performance of the components. An example of component performance is the amount of efficiency that is lost when the cable stretches. It is possible to design into a brake considerable amounts of mechanical advantage; however, every time the mechanical advantage is increased, it will require more length of cable pull to operate the brake, and it will increase the demands on the individual components, primarily the cable and housing system. The available length of cable pull is constrained by the design of the brake lever, which is in turn limited by the size and strength of people's hands.

The roller-cam is a variable mechanical advantage brake which maximises the efficiency of available cable pull. In theory this design puts the greatest mechanical advantage at the point where it counts, i.e., just when the brake shoe contacts the rim. Because of this power range the adjustment is more critical than that of the cantilever, and the rider will obtain the best results by making sure the cable and pad adjustment keeps the brake centred in its power range.

Make adjustments for pad wear by adjusting the pad rather than the cable, because shortening the cable moves the power point of the cam. If the cable is shortened too much, the brake will engage after it passes the power peak, and will be much less efficient. Adjustments for pad wear aren't required that frequently, but riders who have two pairs of wheels with different rim widths may be forced to readjust on changing wheels. Depending on the design of the bike, the model of brake, and the wheel and tyre in use, roller-cams can inhibit wheel changes if they don't open enough to allow the passage of the inflated tyre. Efforts to use shorter chain stays complicate these clearance problems, and on some bikes the rider must deflate the tyre to mount or remove the rear wheel.

Cantilever brakes are not quite linear in their mechanical advantage, because as the brake arm pivots, the tangent formed by the yoke cable moves slightly in relation to the centre of the brake's arc. Although there is a theoretical power peak, for practical purposes performance is linear because the brake travels through a very small arc. This reduces the need for frequent adjustment. To quote Gary Fisher on the subject, 'How often do you even have to think about your cantilever brakes?' Aside from watching for worn pads, not very often.

In some inexpensive 'roller-cams' the bell-shaped cam plate has been eliminated and replaced by a straight-sided trapezoid, which gives the brake a linear power application. This solves some adjustment problems, but loses the variable mechanical advantage of the true cam, which is the idea behind the roller-cam in the first place.

Charlie Cunningham, who helped design the modern roller-cam, has made measurements of mechanical advantage in brake performance. According to his findings the maximum pad pressure exerted by cantilever brakes is in the neighbourhood of 1.5 times the total cable tension. The theoretical limit of pad pressure on roller-cam brakes is about 7 times the cable tension, although in practise the factor is between four and five because the high ratio requires more cable travel than levers can provide. The U-brake has a pad pressure-to-cable tension ratio of about two to one. The mechanical advantage of both the cantilever and U-brake varies with the length of the yoke cable; the shorter the cable, the higher the mechanical advantage.

## Other designs

Cables, cams, and levers are not the only means of transmitting braking power, and this part of the bike is certain to be the focus of scrutiny and experimentation for quite some time. Among the more interesting designs is the hydraulic bicycle brake designed by William Mathauser. It's hard to dismiss the impact hydraulic brakes made on automotive technology, and Mr. Mathauser claims the bicycle version is just as much an improvement as the automotive hydraulic brake was over the 'antique' mechanically operated brake. The major advantage to hydraulic brakes is that they are not subject to the cable stretching and housing compression that is the main loss of efficiency in traditional systems. The weight of the Mathauser brake set is about the same as for a set of Campagnolo road brakes.

Another interesting design is a screw-operated brake. The yoke cable rotates a spring-loaded drum on each side of the rim which turns a worm gear and literally screws down the brakes. One reason this is so interesting is because worm gears are capable of delivering tremendous mechanical advantage. Since the pads on a screw-operated brake travel in a straight line, they do not go out of adjustment as the pads wear down, as do the other types of frame-mounted brakes.

# Riding Techniques

**R**iding on dirt is always a new experience for the uninitiated, but any reasonably athletic rider will find it exhilarating and easy to do on most roads or trails the rider is likely to encounter. Average bike handling skills and a little practice are all it takes.

Still, there are challenges everywhere for mountain bikers of all levels of ability from beginner to expert. Among the situations you will never encounter on paved roads are; riding up steep hills on unpredictable surfaces, riding down same, and dealing with stream crossings, ditches, logs, large rocks, small rocks, and other odd-sized objects. Navigating through such obstacles in an upright posture requires some special techniques in addition to strength and balance. Consider going uphill.

Unpaved roads are often much steeper than anything a road cyclist sees, and they can be littered with obstacles or have uncertain surfaces of loose rock or sand. The limiting factor for uphill riding is not necessarily gearing, because off-roaders use laughable combinations such as a 24-tooth front and a 34-tooth rear for an 18-inch gear. The limits to off-road hill climbing are traction, and the rider's ability to keep the front wheel on the ground.

When you stand up to deliver a powerful pedal stroke, you take weight off the rear wheel, and on a loose surface this can cause the rear wheel to break loose and spin, stalling the bike. Staying in the saddle keeps the wheel from breaking loose by putting more weight on it, and twiddling a tiny gear prevents the power surge that creates a loss of traction.

As the hill gets steeper, redistribute your weight by sliding forward in the saddle to keep the front wheel from lifting and to keep your body weight more directly over the pedals. The problems involved in climbing steep hills have inspired bicycle designs with steeper seat angles and shorter chain stays to get this type of weight distribution. Riders who ride without toe clips and straps can even move their feet forward on the pedal to get a little more leg extension and to move the weight a little farther forward. Of course, this doesn't work for riders who use toe clips and straps, which is an increasingly popular set up.

Under racing conditions it is sometimes more efficient to use the 24-inch, or 2-foot gear; in other words, to pick up the bike and hoof it up the hill. But on casual rides with no emphasis on speed, riders enjoy the challenge of trying to ride all the way up each hill, no matter how steep, without stopping, in what amounts to uphill Observed Trials. In doing this it is important that you pace yourself on the easy parts of the slope to conserve your energy for the steep pitches or rough spots. As slope and road surface conditions permit, stand up to rest the muscle groups you use while sitting, then when the going gets tougher, sit down and speed up your spin so your momentum will carry you through ditches or over large rocks. If the road is wide enough, you can take a longer and less steep route by tacking back and forth.

There are two ways of getting down hills, 'in control' and 'more fun'. Like skiing, the gravity-fed potential of mountain biking is inescapable. But while skiers are confined to resorts, mountain bikers share roads and trails with many other users, and this is certainly the most sensitive and emotional area of conflict between mountain bikers and the anti-bike forces. That said, there are still times when a rapid trip down the mountain is appropriate.

Before we look at high-performance downhill, let's look at control. On some very steep, rough, or slippery descents riders will have to travel very slowly. On these tricky 'trials' downhills, beginning riders characteristically dangle one foot while the other holds the pedal at the lowest point. Although this works if the rider overbalances to the side with the extremity dangling, a fall to the other side is disaster because the foot is glued to the pedal. This awkward position also reduces the shock-absorbing capacity of the knees, as well as reducing ground clearance.

Proper technique here involves keeping the cranks horizontal and standing with equal weight on each pedal. This allows the rider to hold his body higher over the saddle and makes room to take up shock by flexing the knees. With both pedals up, ground clearance is maximised, and balancing the weight over the bike makes manoeuvres to either side equally easy (or equally difficult, depending on point of view). With the saddle lowered and your weight well back, you can easily ride down a flight of stairs.

One of the hardest types of obstacles to deal with is one encountered on a steep downhill, either a ditch or a log. The rider is usually pulling hard on the front brake, which shifts weight forward and makes it difficult to lighten the front wheel enough to lift it over the problem area. Timing is important, because the rider must release the front brake to pull the wheel up, and on a steep hill this will cause the bike to accelerate. As soon as the front wheel is past the obstacle, shift the weight forward and press down on the bars to minimise impact on the rear wheel. By now the bike will be travelling considerably faster, and it will be time to grab a double handful of brakes.

**Descending: keep the cranks levels and your weight well back.**

On descents the front brake must be treated with respect. If it is applied in a curve it can wash out the front wheel, and if applied when the front wheel drops into a hole it can cause the rider to perform a stunt that mountain bikers cheerfully call the 'face-plant'. Even worse, it can cause damage to fork or frame. Under most downhill conditions it is a good idea to keep your hand off the front brake lever except when it is in active use. Using your rear brake to control your speed, you can grasp the handlebar firmly with your front brake hand, reducing the possibility of losing your grip on a paint-shaker downhill. For high-speed cornering, racers go as far into a corner as possible before applying brakes, then grab a lot of front brake while still travelling in a straight line, easing off as the bike starts to lean into the curve.

A common practice on the part of those setting up a bike is to adjust the brake so that it engages at the first touch of the lever. This means that in order to grasp the lever, you must either open your hand, or brake with two fingers, which reduces the grip on the handlebar. This may be especially tough on people with small hands. I set my brake up so it engages with the lever closer to the handlebar, and it reaches maximum braking as it reaches the end of the cable travel.

One advanced technique for rapid cornering flies in the face of most riders' instincts. The usual practice is for the rider to keep the outside pedal at its lowest point through the corner, with the inside foot off the pedal and poised for a 'stab' at the ground for support in case of a skid. The advanced technique places the inside pedal down and slightly to the rear of centre to keep it from dragging. This shifts the rider's weight to the inside, keeping the bike more upright, in the manner of motorcycle racers who hang almost to the ground on the insides of corners. This also cocks the pedal for the first pedal stroke coming out of the corner. Of course, this should only be done by helmeted riders on an approved course under adult supervision.

Now we come to the go-slow obstacles. Taken to its logical extreme and then extended somewhat farther, this end of the mountain bike skill has evolved into a sport known as Observed Trials. To this end, bike makers have designed bikes that are far more acrobatic than they are strictly 'mountain bikes', i.e., built for off-road exploring. The line between mountain bikes and 'trials' bikes is not clearly defined. Most mountain bikes can be used in Observed Trials, the more specifically the bike is designed for performance in this area, the more can be done with it.

Obstacles such as logs and rocks can be fun. The large chainring is 8 or 9 nine inches off the ground, so this represents the practical limit to the size of the obstacle that can be cleared (some riders will take on larger ones if the chain is on the large ring to protect the gear teeth). Approaching such an obstacle, pull the front up into a 'wheelie' until the front wheel clears, then throw your weight forward to pull the rear wheel up and over.

The most advanced method for clearing small obstacles is called the 'bunny hop' by its inventors, BMX brats who didn't realise that it is impossible to pull both wheels off the ground while attached only by the handlebars. While this manoeuvre can be performed with toe clips and straps, it was invented without them and is more a matter of balance and weight shifting than it is of actually pulling upward on the bike. On their little bikes, BMXers can clear dustbins or saw benches with a jump from level ground without using toe clips and straps. For larger bikes the limits are a little lower because there is less room over the top tube for the rider to pull the bike up. The bunny hop is a matter of speed and delicate timing, since the rider must be travelling fast enough for both wheels to clear the obstacle before he comes down. The consequences of jumping too early or too late are too horrible to contemplate.

Set up for the bunny hop by standing with cranks horizontal and your weight balanced between them. Flexing your knees, spring upward, pulling up on the bars at the same time. Just as the front wheel begins to lift, push forward, which rotates the bike around its centre of gravity and pulls up the rear wheel. Bend your knees again and 'suck' the bike even further up, and then as the bike comes down, straighten your legs and push down on the pedals to keep your feet on them and prepare for the shock of landing. Easy, n'est ce pas? The manoeuvre takes considerably less time to perform than it does to describe. One tip: practise on the street before you attempt to clear a log!

For obstacles that can't be ridden over, off-roaders can use a technique perfected by cyclo-crossers. Approaching the obstacle, the rider swings his leg over the bike and coasts the last few yards while standing on the left pedal. At the same time he releases the right grip and grasps the top tube with the right hand. Stepping through with his right foot between the left foot and the bike, he picks up the bike and uses his momentum to help him vault the obstacle. If this is done properly, the left pedal will stay at the bottom of its arc in position for the remount, and the rider will have preserved his forward momentum.

Now and then you will encounter an obstacle that can't be ridden over, hopped, or jumped, such as a washout, a landslide, or a short cut, and for these you'll need to carry the bike. Although there are a number of ways to do it, most of them preclude scrambling over rocks and logs. The proper technique is also borrowed from cyclo-cross, a sport whose participants seem to enjoy carrying the bike more than they do riding it. Standing on the left side of the bike (away from the greasy drive elements), put your right arm through the frame and grasp the stem or handlebar. The bike rests on your shoulder in the angle formed by the top and seat tubes, while your right hand controls the balance of the bike. The left hand is free for balancing as well as for grasping at straws, tree roots, or a helping hand.

There are now several versions of straps or pads which can make this method of carrying more comfortable; at the same time, a seat post-mounted water bottle cage makes it more difficult to pick up the bike. For larger frame sizes there are webbing shoulder slings, but for small frame sizes the sling takes up so much room that it's hard to get an arm between the water bottle and the sling. Shorter riders can get around this by padding the tubes; there are several manufacturers making special frame pads.

Water crossings are one of the prime spectator areas of any mountain bike ride. Everyone stops to see who is going for a swim. You can ride through streams up to a foot deep if you concentrate on avoiding rocks, maintaining traction, and ignoring the water pouring in over the tops of your boots. Approaching the water hazard, slow down and shift into a low gear to keep from bogging down and stalling in the middle. Keeping your weight on the saddle for traction, look for the shallowest area, and take your chances.

Because of the width of the tyre, the limitations of travel of the front derailleur, and the technical aspects of chain line, when the bike is in the lowest gear the chain travels very close to the tyre. This is not a problem on the uphill, but on the downhill it can be. There will be a lot of slack in the chain, and a worn spring in the derailleur cage will reduce chain tension even more; the bike may also be bouncing over a rough surface. The result is that the chain can catch on the side knobs of the tyre and get sucked in between the chain stay and the tyre, scratching the paint, scarring the chain stay, twisting the chain, and incidentally stopping all forward progress.

One method of dealing with the problem after it strikes is to stop, get off, and rotate the rear wheel backwards. An experienced rider can clear the chain quickly by momentarily hitting the brake to lock the rear wheel, while at the same time applying forward pressure on the cranks. As soon as the chain pops out, the brakes are released, and the entire manoeuvre takes a fraction of a second.

Home-made chain guards that prevent this problem have been around for some time, and now the manufacturers are bringing out products along the same lines. A typical home-made device to keep the chain clear is simply a section of fine wire running from a point on the chain stay next to the tyre to the seat tube at the derailleur clamp.

In the absence of such a device, riding technique can be helpful in preventing 'chain

**Water crossings: gear down—and take your chances!**

suck'. As the rider crests the top of a climb, he shifts from the small chainring onto either the middle or outer chainring. This gives the chain more tension, and moves it away from the tyre.

Conditions of slope change rapidly during off-road rides, and a descent can turn suddenly into a momentary ascent of a steep cliff. Failure to shift in time leads to bogging down in too high a gear when the chain speed becomes so slow that a shift is no longer possible. This is usually accompanied by crunching noises from the rear derailleur and followed by the sound of muted cursing.

One way the rider can improve his technique dramatically is with a little indoor practice. Bicycle rollers may be the most boring form of exercise ever invented, but they can do wonders for off-road form. For the purpose of improving form, 'wind-load' bike trainers are a bust. You want the kind that you can fall off, with three turning drums rather than the kind that the bike bolts into, because the point is not exercise but skill, and if you can't fall off, you won't learn anything.

Since off-road bikes usually have longer wheelbases than road bikes, your mountain bike may be too long to ride a set of rollers effectively; rather than sitting on top of the front roller, the front wheel may hang over the front end. If this is the case, you can get the same training on a road bike.

What we are attempting to do is to develop a smooth circular pedal stroke, and to increase the spin rate. Improvement in these areas will make a dramatic difference in the rider's ability to get up steep hills. The faster the spin rate, the smoother the application of power; as the rider's spin slows down there is a pronounced dead spot as well as a power surge, and where traction is limited the power surge will break the rear tyre loose. By maintaining a higher spin rate in a lower gear at the same speed, the rider can stay in the saddle where he can control traction more effectively.

We'll skip the basic roller instructions; any reasonably skilled rider can learn to ride them in a short time. Since the rollers are to be used more to improve form than to increase aerobic capacity, there is no need for hour-long, sweat-drenched roller sessions. Considering how boring roller riding is, twenty minutes at a time ought to be enough, and three or four sessions of this length a season is enough to polish the technique.

The object is to increase the spin rate, so it is not necessary to ride in the highest gear; in fact, the lower the gear, the more effective the exercise because there is less resistance on the pedals. After a couple of minutes of easy warm up on the rollers, increase your spin rate to the point where the rear wheel becomes difficult to control. You will find that as you hit your maximum rate, the rear of the bike begins to bounce around. Back off until the rear wheel becomes steady, then gradually increase the cadence, concentrating on keeping your body motionless and the rear wheel steady. At maximum spin rate, you will have to let up shortly, but you will begin to feel how your body movement affects the bike.

A series of 'intervals', sprints alternating with slow riding, is the most effective way to improve form. A twenty-minute roller session can't really do much in terms of fitness, but the feedback the rider gets does wonders for quieting body movement, and the results in terms of improved performance may be just as dramatic as the results of increased aerobic capacity. In effect, by increasing his maximum spin rate, the rider widens the range of each gear, and by learning to quiet his body movement, he gets the most out of limited traction. In addition, learning to ride rollers is excellent practice in bicycle control and handling.

# Clothing and Accessories

When it came to clothes, the early mountain bike riders rarely wore cycling clothing, except for a few who wore bike jerseys. Jeans and T-shirts were the rule, with boots instead of cycling shoes. In 1982 a Japanese magazine published an article that attempted to describe mountain biking to the Japanese readership. An artist's illustration pointed out the California clothing style, obviously drawn from a photo and easily recognizable as Gary Fisher. Captions and pointers carefully pointed out and identified the baseball cap, the jeans, the heavy boots, the leather gloves, the long-sleeved wool shirt and down bodywarmer as typical California mountain bike clothing; of course this combination of clothing also wouldn't be unusual for anyone in northern California who went out into the woods on a winter day for any reason.

At a typical NORBA mountain bike race the clothing has reached the other end of the spectrum. For one thing, since helmets are mandatory, hard-shells have replaced baseball caps as the head gear of choice. (The increase in helmet consciousness may be one of the more important contributions of racing.) Team riders wear form-fitting matching outfits in the often garish colours popular with road racers. Much of the time the clothing is an ordinary bicycle racing outfit straight off the bike shop rack, because under competitive conditions mountain bike racers need the same type of cooling and comfort that road racers do.

Lycra has replaced wool as the most popular material for bike clothing, and whatever the other aspects of its performance, this material is not very resistant to abrasion, and practically melts if the rider hits the dirt. Even if the rider doesn't fall off during a ride, the off-road environment has plenty of abrasive elements, and for this reason a little more rugged material is indicated. Manufacturers would love mountain bikers to carefully define the ideal clothing, but conditions of mountain bike use vary so widely that it isn't that easy. Some can get away with the lightest Lycra outfit, while others will need arctic gear.

As I pointed out in the touring section, the key to mountain bike clothing is having enough to keep warm under the most extreme conditions the rider is likely to encounter. On an autumn day this may mean taking an extra windbreaker, and on a winter day it might mean packing a down jacket, spare socks, and extra gloves. You can't count on the fact that you are moving to keep warm, since mechanical problems or injuries can bring everything to a halt. In the case of an injury, someone may need extra warmth. The point is that you never have to worry about being too hot on a cold day, so take more clothing than you need.

On a cold day mountain bikers have the same requirements as road cyclists, i.e., keeping the body temperature constant while the external temperature and the rate of activity fluctuate. Standard wisdom is that the rider should dress in layers, and try to prevent overheating by removing one at a time as the activity generates heat. Sweaty inner garments can be cold, another reason to avoid overheating, although some cycling clothing made of new synthetic materials wicks the moisture away from the body to prevent this problem.

Before the introduction of shoes designed for mountain biking, the most popular type of foot gear at off-road events was one of several versions of light hiking boot, either high cut or low cut, made of Goretex and leather. The sole had enough grip for hiking excursions away from the bike, and the boot was light enough for comfortable riding.

Problems with rough-soled shoes arise if the rider wants to use toe clips, an increasingly popular option, because such shoes don't slip in and out of the clips easily.

The bicycle and shoe industries have given us a variety of mountain bike shoes, some similar to the shoes originally popular but with an indented tread for use with toe clips, and others following the lines of traditional cycle touring shoes. The most significant difference in shoe types is whether or not they have stiff soles. Stiffness is essential to some extent, but a completely rigid sole like that on a road racing shoe begins to interfere with walking. If the rider has few occasions to get off the bike, such as in a race, stiff soles are the way to go. For rides that include walking, a sole that bends in the middle is much more comfortable.

Wet feet are unavoidable on rides that include stream crossings; no amount of waterproofing of the foot gear keeps feet dry when water pours in over the tops. The only help here is a spare pair of dry shoes and socks. This is a lesson I learned from the Crested Butte to Aspen tour, because on a cool night at 11,000 feet wet shoes are misery. An indelible impression of the camp site on that tour was the unmistakable aroma of burning Vibram soles and wool socks around the camp fire.

Either touring or racing style shorts are adequate for mountain biking, but knickerbockers and knee socks, even with gaiters, are a good alternative, especially as the weather turns cooler. Mountain bike trousers have padded knees, but in my experience this is more helpful in keeping the knees warm than it is as protection against falls.

**Helmets are now accepted apparel**

I'm a bit of a reactionary, and as often as not I'll be seen riding my mountain bike in blue jeans, which always shocks my more proper bikie friends. Perhaps by clinging to the original clothing style I'm attempting to tell the world that I still don't take this fat tyre nonsense seriously.

# Accessories

Mountain bikes have spawned a long list of accessories designed to make the rider's life easier. In this area the garage inventors are still active, and at any given moment hundreds of mountain bikers are probably in the workshop filing, bending, welding, or sewing their ideas together.

As I mentioned in the touring section, manufacturers have redesigned their packs and racks for off-road use. In addition to the standard sets of panniers, mountain bikers can also choose from bags and tool kits that mount on their triangulated handlebars, under the saddle, or inside the main triangle of the frame.

The bottle cage might seem like an item that needs no adaptation for mountain bikes, but any tough race will see the trail littered with bottles that bounced out of their cages. For rougher roads and especially with the new larger water bottles, a heavy-duty mountain bike bottle cage is a good idea.

The patented Hite-Rite seat relocator spring is one accessory that is standard equipment on many of the fancier stock models and on most race bikes. The Hite-Rite comes in several lengths giving different amounts of seat post adjustment. To operate the Hite-Rite the rider loosens the seat post quick-release and uses his weight to lower the saddle. To raise it back to the predetermined height, he loosens the quick-release and the saddle pops back to the correct height, lined up with the frame. The manufacturers also point out that the Hite-Rite makes it harder for anyone to steal the saddle from a parked bike.

Carrying a loaded bike can be uncomfortable without a shoulder sling that mounts in the main triangle in the angle of the seat cluster. Some of the slings on the market include a tool pouch. Riders with smaller frames may find that there is no room for an arm between the sling and the bottle cage, and these people will be happier with a set of connected pads that wrap around the seat and top tubes.

A pump is a necessary accessory, and riders can choose from those made for road bikes or an ultra-light version. The smaller a pump, the easier it is to carry, but the longer it will take to inflate a tyre. For riders with time on their hands and limited space, there are pumps only a few inches long that weigh less than three ounces. An alternative to carrying a pump that is favoured by racers is the use of cartridge inflators; these are either the type that also injects a latex compound to seal the leak or a simple pressurized cylinder. Obviously, these are one-shot devices, and it is a good idea to carry refills.

If the pump tip is allowed to collect mud, it can inject dirt into the tyre valve when it is used. This can keep the valve from closing properly and gives the same effect as a slow leak. Cover the pump tip, and use valve caps on your tyres.

Lighting for night riding is an area that is receiving considerable attention. Power can be supplied by either batteries or a dynamo, and both have their advantages and drawbacks. The main problem with batteries is weight. In terms of performance, the gel-cell rechargeable battery is best, but it is the heaviest. Ni-Cad rechargeable batteries are lighter, but they are more expensive, and when they fail they tend to fail abruptly, while the gel-cell just gets dimmer. If a Ni-Cad battery is drained too much it will be damaged. The average battery system will operate for several hours before it needs recharging, which is enough for casual rides if not for tours.

Dynamos are lightweight, but the rider must supply the power from his own muscles. They also stop when the bike does, a problem that has mountain bikers mounting them on the front wheel so the light doesn't quit if the rider locks the brakes! Perhaps the best alternative would be a battery system that is recharged by the bicycle dynamo; such systems are increasing in availability.

Helmet mounted lights have the advantage that the light shines wherever the rider looks, but because the light source is so close to the rider's eyes, there are no visible shadows. This gives everything a flat, depthless look that can be confusing and can make a rough road look smooth. These lights are more effective when used along with a handlebar mounted system that gives a better impression of the road surface.

Speaking of helmets, this is another important accessory. The United States and several other countries have adopted standards for bicycle helmet impact performance. These standards have raised the quality of bicycle helmets, and the old leather 'hair net' helmet is history because it did not measure up. Hard-shell helmets are now mandatory at all competitive mountain bike events and on some packaged tours.

The only problem with the helmet standards is that helmets are tested for impact and retention only, not for comfort, and some riders might find the most effective helmet too uncomfortable, heavy, and hot to wear. A helmet that is left at home for these reasons does the rider no good at all. Before buying a helmet, make sure it is one you want to wear all the time, not just at races.

A skid-plate isn't a vital piece of equipment for everyone, but this item can prevent damage to chainrings and permit new levels of Observed Trials performance or even casual riding. Skid-plates are either home-made or manufactured components that attach to the frame and protect the outer chainwheel from logs or rocks. Trials riders use their skid-plates to rock their bikes over large obstacles.

A digital speedometer certainly won't make a ride any easier, but it will tell you how hard you worked. Depending on how much you are willing to spend, one of these ultra-light gadgets will tell you (in addition to your current speed), the date and time of day, your average speed, distance travelled, whether you are ahead or behind a predetermined pace, your pedalling cadence, and your pulse rate. Next year's model will also compute your age and telephone bill.

It is not necessarily an item of faith that chainrings have to be round. In 1976 I experimented with an elliptical gear on my mountain bike, but while the ellipse seemed effective at low-speed climbing, it was too extreme to permit a decent spin rate, and I abandoned it. Shimano has introduced the patented and trade-marked Bio-Pace chainring, which is not round or elliptical but has a complex computer designed shape with three axes of varying length. The idea is to extract maximum efficiency from the rider with slightly varying gear ratios that correspond to the strengths and weaknesses of the rider's circular pedal stroke. The effect is more pronounced in the lower gears, and reduced in the large chainrings to make it easier for the rider to maintain a high-speed spin on the road.

# Thin Air Repairs

For the mountain biker the health of the machine can be of paramount importance. On the road a cyclist with a damaged bike is not usually in immediate danger, because unless the road is extremely remote, a vehicle will be along sooner or later, and if the occupant is not willing to offer a lift, at least he can carry news of the cyclist's plight.

Mountain bikers on recreational outings may be more severely inconvenienced by damaged machinery. Depending on the nature of the damage, the rider may have to abandon the ride and hike with the bike a considerable distance to get home or to find a repair facility.

On rides of a less recreational nature, such as an exploration of the Himalayas, the rider's very life depends on the bike's continued good health. Rugged as they are, mountain bikes are subject to the same types of mundane damage that occur to road bikes under considerably less stress. Derailleurs can be twisted, chains can break, pedals or cranks can snap, and even the frame can be broken.

Most mountain bikers have enough sense to take a minimum set of tools with them on rugged outings, along with a pump, spare tube, and a patch kit. A number of published sources have described the tools the cyclist will need to perform simple repairs; these include a small adjustable spanner, hex-keys, screwdrivers, and a chain tool.

But sometimes things happen that are outside the scope of such a tool kit. On my bicycle exploration of the Northwest Territories our group carried spare tyres, derailleurs, cables, and miscellaneous small hardware. During the trip the only repairs performed were an adjustment of the derailleur cables on one bike, and the replacement of one of the screws that had rattled out of a rear rack.

One of the members of our expedition, Al Farrell, had considerable bicycle touring experience, and it was he who had brought along the handful of spare screws that were used to repair the rack. The reason he had this hardware in the first place went back to a previous ride where he had found himself in a remote area with a flapping rack and no replacement screws. In true mountain bike repair fashion, he found that the screws that held the cleats on his cycling shoes fitted the rack perfectly.

From the earliest days of the clunker movement, mountain bikers have exhibited an ability to conduct nearly miraculous repairs under trying conditions, using for materials whatever is at hand. The primary clunker tool during the seventies was a pair of Vise-Grips clamped onto the seat post; the secondary clunker tool was a Swiss Army knife, preferably the kind that bristles with files, hack-saw blades, and screwdrivers. With these two tools nearly any repair could be improvised.

Inventive repairs are a natural outgrowth of the mentality it took during the mid-seventies to have a clunker, which was not really a mountain bike in the modern sense, but a customised bike built on a frame that might be as much as fifty years old. The first experimental bikes were nowhere near as reliable as those of the present day, and any group ride was likely to see a breakdown of one kind or another. Before I made the switch from rebuilt clunkers to a modern hand-built mountain bike frame, I personally destroyed at least one specimen of every component on my bike. The damage that I and my friends were doing to our cycling equipment was almost a standing joke, and we considered putting together a complete bike from all the broken parts we had collected. In fact, one of the reasons I started thinking about custom frames sometime around 1976 was that by this time I was only getting about six months out of one of the old frames that were becoming increasingly hard too find.

Clunker bikes weren't available at any bike shops, they had to be made, either by the owner or by one of the few bike mechanics who had the esoteric parts available and was familiar with the standard 'Marin County' conversion. Some parts had to be made or modified, and all the custom work left open possibilities for repairs and adjustments the average bike owner knew nothing about. Drum brake linings had to be checked, or coaster brakes had to be freshly greased on nearly every ride. Old components, especially filed, sawn, and re-bent old components, are not the most reliable, and riders knew that in spite of their bikes' rugged aspects, it was always a good idea for them to care lovingly for their machinery. Remember that at this point we only used the bikes in the hills in the vicinity of our homes, so at worst if a bike gave up completely, the rider might have to hike four or five miles. Still, we made every effort to get the bike back if a repair could be effected.

On one occasion, a rider suffered from a complete collapse of the front wheel while with a group of friends enjoying the sunset from the top of a prominent local hill. Since the way back was all downhill, a repair was created by spreading the forks on the damaged bike and bolting them to the rear axle of another bike. This created a three-wheel tandem, which was successfully ridden to the conclusion of the ride, although the rear rider found he had to lean the opposite direction on turns.

Because the heavy Uniroyal balloon tyres in use during the seventies rarely went flat, few riders carried pumps or patch kits. Of course, Murphy's Law ('Anything that can go wrong, will go wrong') is alive and well, and now and then a rider would be faced with the problem of a flat tyre. On many occasions the problem was dealt with by stuffing the tyre full of grass, which gave a rough ride and was hard on the rim. Because drum brakes were the rule on these bikes, even the most severely bent rim didn't affect braking too much.

Modern mountain biking equipment has gone a long way toward relieving riders of the necessity for such ingenuity. Bikes are standardised, so parts are now inter-changeable; ten years of experimentation has pin-pointed most of the likely problem areas, so riders can be equipped to deal with common problems. Still, the nature of the sport is such that now and then riders must concoct repairs out of thin air.

Because mountain bikers may not need to repair tyres for considerable lengths of time, the patch kit is carried but sometimes neglected. Now and then a rider will break out the tyre kit for the first time in a year, only to find that all the glue has evaporated. One rider came up with an ingenious method for repairing a flat with a pump but no patch kit. In desperation, he twisted the tube around a stick at the point of the leak, sealing off the affected section. Putting everything back together, tyre, tube, stick and all, he pumped it up, and rode home with no further problems.

Many riders have had occasion to stuff a flat tyre full of grass. This may not give a comfortable ride, but it can get the bike back without damage to the rim.

An Idaho mountain biker tells me that the hollow end of his seat post has served as a vital repair tool on several occasions. In one instance he used it to straighten a bent drop-out, and in another he used it to straighten a bent brake pivot. He also mentioned that on one occasion he used it as a hammer, but after consideration of the damage he no longer recommends this.

On an expedition down the back roads of the Mexican province of Baja California, one of my friends violated one of the paramount rules of mountain biking, which is, 'if it ain't broke, don't fix it'. Annoyed by a noise in his crankset, he attempted to tighten the crank arm bolt, and succeeded only in destroying it. With about 100 miles to go in the expedition, he was faced with the prospect of riding with one leg. One of the other riders jokingly suggested that he use the bolt out of the other crank arm. Joke or not, this turned out to be the solution. The rider pulled the good bolt and put it in the loose crank arm. He rode until the other crank arm came loose, and then reversed the process. Silly as it sounds, the repair had to be repeated only about every 30 miles, and allowed the rider to complete the distance.

My favourite thin air repair took place near Crested Butte, while I was riding with a couple of friends on a dirt road a few miles out of town. My friend Larry had the misfortune to lose one of the the hex-keyed axle bolts from his front hub. As we stopped to examine the situation, it seemed obvious that he couldn't ride with this problem, because it put a severe strain on one fork blade and affected his braking. We reasoned that he might snap the fork blade with regrettable consequences if he continued that way.

We quickly established that none of the three of us was carrying the necessary obscure

**Beyond help**

spare part, and in typical mountain bike fashion, we started searching our immediate environs for materials with which to concoct a repair. There was a rusty barbed-wire fence, a raw material that has been used in numerous off-road repairs, but we couldn't think of an application. The few trees in the area were stunted pines whose soft, splintery wood was of no use. Then, about 15 feet off the road, I spotted the broken end of a shovel handle, probably discarded by a rancher. This was the toughest piece of weathered ash anyone could ask for, the perfect raw material.

My friend Howie got to work with his Swiss Army knife, and carefully carved the splintered end of the handle into a blunt, tapered point about the size of the missing screw. Using the end of the handle as a screwdriver, he forced it into the threaded end of the axle; the hard wood threaded itself perfectly. Then, Howie used the wood saw on his knife to sever the new screw from the rest of the handle, and *voila!*, instant axle screw. The repair got Larry safely home, and the makeshift screw now occupies a small plaque on his mantelpiece.

**Wende Cragg**

# Women
# and
# Mountain Bikes

In the beginning of the movement, roughly the mid-seventies, there were few women involved in the sport of mountain biking. This was due in part to the fact that it was quite a trick to get a mountain bike together in the first place. Perhaps because of the cultural climate of the time, certainly not out of any desire on the part of the male participants to keep mountain bikes a male sport, there were few women who had the inclination or the facility to go to the extremes it took to own a clunker bike. I can remember many evenings sitting around with a half-dozen clunker riders, all male, bemoaning the fact that we had taken up a sport with no women in it.

One woman who did get past the cultural and mechanical barriers, and who deserves the title of the pioneer female mountain biker, is Wende Cragg of Fairfax, California. Wende took up the sport almost in self-defence, since her husband and all her male neighbours had gone crazy modifying old bikes. Once she announced her desire to participate, she was provided with equipment by a few men who hoped that this spark of female acceptance of off-roading might be fanned into a little more of a flame.

The off-road cycling equipment of the era may also have had something to do with the absence of women in the respect that it was so heavy. Wende's 1976 state-of-the-art clunker was still about 50 pounds of inefficiency, nearly half her body weight and a severe disadvantage for her compared to the men when clunker 'rides' often involved long trudging pushes up steep grades.

In an era when the only real racing was the Repack downhill, the women who were aware at all of off-road riding perceived it as a macho cowboy sport about as refined as seeing who could hold his hand over a candle the longest. For comparison, BMX, which is equally available to riders of both sexes, has far more male participants than

**Jacquie Phelan, three-times NORBA U.S. National Champion, competing in the 1985 Man v Horse v Mountain Bike race at Llanwrytd Wells, Wales.**

female. During this era women's participation in bicycle road racing was growing rapidly, and women from the United States are regarded as being among the best in the world in this part of the sport.

Wende Cragg took up photography about the same time she took up cycling, and she and her husband Larry Cragg helped capture on film the spirit of the times that no-one realised would be so fleeting. Her title as the pioneer woman in mountain biking should be confirmed by the fact that she was the first woman to own a modern mountain bike, one of Joe Breeze's first ten in 1978. Wende was also one of only two women to participate in the Repack Downhill race before 1980, the first time in 1976 (the other, Donna Degen, raced for her first time one year later). Another first contributed by Wende Cragg was her participation in the 1979 National U.S. Cyclo-Cross Championships, the only woman to finish, although she was denied a national championship jersey because the promoters felt that the low level of female participation did not justify the granting of a national title. Wende was also the first woman to ride over Pearl Pass on the famous Crested Butte tour.

Since the mountain bike has been refined and made as available as any other piece of recreational equipment, women are taking up the sport with enthusiasm and in ever-increasing numbers. Certainly the outlaw bicyclist image has been completely shed, and the image of the mountain bike rider is no more extreme than that of a cross-country skier. Women are even beginning to turn up on mountain bikes in commercials for products which are unrelated to bicycles, but which use the healthy outdoor image as a selling point.

If a group of men announced that they were putting on a ride in which women were not permitted, they might find themselves picketed by representatives of several local women's groups; conversely, all-women rides have found enthusiastic acceptance. Female-only rides have become part of the Crested Butte Bike Week, and several female tour operators have held all-female off-road tours.

In such groups women beginners can explore the sport without the distraction of the group of male riders that is always seeing who can be first to the peak. Certainly women have this element, shown by racing performance, but it doesn't seem to be a factor on group rides as much as it is with men. Women find that without men in the group they can be considerably more candid in their discussions. (I'm not making this up. I have female friends who have infiltrated such groups.)

At mountain bike races the women's field is still a fraction of the men's, but women's off-road racing has arrived, and the women give nothing away to the men in terms of toughness. Jacquie Phelan, the U.S. women's mountain bike champion for the first three years of national competition, was rarely challenged during her first three seasons, and instead of comparing her performance to the other women, who were not yet in her class, she compared her performance to that of the top men; she habitually finished in the middle of the expert men's field.

One of the stories to come out of women's racing is certain to endure as a legend of mountain biking, perhaps a legend of cycling in general.

It happened in one of the toughest mountain bike races of 1986, a race that climbed

**Look, no saddle. Cindy Whitehead rode 49 miles of a 50-mile race through the Sierras sans saddle—and still won.**

and descended 7,500 feet over 50 miles of rough and sandy road, from the Owens Valley of California at 5,000 feet elevation to 11,000 feet in the Sierra Nevada mountains and back. In the women's race the challenge was between three-time U.S. national champion Jacquie Phelan and her arch-rival Cindy Whitehead. A win by either would not be unusual, since in two previous meetings that year they had split the honours.

Not far from the start, about a mile into the race, Cindy felt her saddle coming loose. When she stopped to inspect the problem, she discovered that the binder bolt in the seat post had broken and her saddle was about to fall off. Of course, the sensible and reasonable thing to do would be to quit on the spot, but had she done so the incident would not be worth writing about.

Realizng that she had no chance, Cindy quickly decided to ride part of the course to get in a little training and then quit at a check-point. Discarding the saddle, she took a patch kit and her car keys from her saddlebag and stuffed them into her jersey pocket. 'I could just see myself after the race, wandering around in the desert looking for my car keys,' she said later. Leaving the seat post sticking dangerously out of the frame ('I tried to get it out but it was stuck, and Jacquie was riding up the road. . . .'), Cindy got back on her bike and took up the pursuit.

To her surprise she caught up with Jacquie, who had figured her to be out of the picture and took the opportunity to loaf a bit. Now the race was on again, and to some extent the toughness of the course worked in Cindy's behalf. The last brutal climb was 3,000 feet in 3 miles, at high altitude, and both were forced to push their bikes, so the absence of the saddle didn't matter. Cindy pulled away from Jacquie for a clear advantage at the start of the downhill.

But the race was a long way from over, and Cindy had 20 miles of descent still to do on sandy roads with the dangerously exposed seat post. As it turned out, both riders fell on the descent, and Phelan suffered more injury with a twisted ankle. Cindy even had a flat and was forced to use the only supplies she had brought, her patch kit, before finishing the most satisfying win of her life in just over six hours. Consider what it takes to win a race without being able to sit for that length of time.

As the awards were handed out, every one of the male riders present, a group that included the best and the toughest of their time, acknowledged that he couldn't have and wouldn't have done what Cindy Whitehead had done.

# Access
# to the
# Wilderness

The land access issue boils down to one or the other: there are places mountain bikers can go, and places where they are not permitted. In the UK all land is owned, whether it is either private or public. The issue for mountain bike adventurers isn't so much who owns the land but whether they have a right of way across it.

Since there are more than 100,000 miles of paths and unmetalled tracks that criss-cross Britain, some sort of instant guide is essential. The best, without doubt, are Ordnance Survey maps. The pink 1:50,000 Landranger series shows rights of way marked in red as well as roads and railways. OS maps also provide unrivalled information about the contours of the landscape, show woodland and forests, rivers, streams, lakes and reservoirs, railway stations, churches, post offices and pubs. On the larger scale 1:25,000 OS Pathfinder maps the three types of public path open to mountain bikes – bridleways, RUPPs (roads used as public paths) and byways open to all traffic – are shown as green dotted and ticked lines. OS maps are as up to date as the day they are printed (shown on the imprint) and are revised regularly. But changes may have occurred since, so it is possible that a right of way may have been extinguished. This is not common, but if you are planning an expedition to a specific area or trying to establish a long-distance off-road route then you will need to study the Definitive Maps of an area. These are available for public inspection and are held by the county surveyors in England and Wales and regional surveyors in Scotland. The maps are up to ten times as detailed as the Pathfinder series and, as their name implies, define the legal status of all rights of way and land boundaries.

The most common rights of way are footpaths and bridleway. Footpaths present problems. Many are feasible for riding on but you have no legal right to do so. Even if the local council has not passed a law prohibiting or restricting riding on the footpath you may still be committing a technical offence. The right to cycle on a bridleway, which is defined as a way over which there is a public right on foot or horseback, with a right to drive animals, is enshrined in s.30 of the 1968 Countryside Act. However cyclists must give way to walkers and horseriders. Not all bridleways, however, are open to cyclists. Local authorities have the power to ban cycling on them but must signpost any such restriction.

That some local authorities are prepared to do so is an indication of the hostility that has always existed in some areas towards cyclists and is now regrettably being exacerbated by the explosion in the use of mountain bikes. In the U.S. the issue of whether mountain bike riders should have access to areas such as green belt, open space, National Parks, Wilderness Areas and National Forests, has become known as the access to the wilderness issue. UK riders are beginning to experience similar problems. The Three Peaks in the Yorkshire Dales, the Quantocks and Burnham Beeches are now all out of bounds for competitive mountain bike riding.

The objections to mountain bikers follow two basic themes. First, the media's attention to the gonzo elements of mountain biking, and the obvious potential for abuse, have given the sport an image problem. Walkers and horseriders do not want to feel in danger of their lives on a narrow trail, and unfortunately more than a few have suffered from collisions or near misses. This type of incident will get more publicity than any number of pleasant encounters, and even if irresponsible riders constitute a minority of those involved with mountain bikes, no amount of effort on the part of responsible cyclists will change the opinion of a walker who has had an unpleasant meeting with a mountain biker.

The second major objection comes from environmentalists who feel that a bicycle is an unwelcome intrusion of civilisation in remote rural areas. This argument is more emotional than the first, since it hinges on the exact amount of civilisation that should be permitted in these areas. Certainly none of the anti-cycling elements is ready to suggest that backpackers abandon all their civilised technology such as their internal frame back packs, Swiss army knives, butane stoves, and even fancy outdoor clothing!

I don't believe that mountain bikes are appropriate in every setting, but I don't feel that they should be equated with motorcycles and 4-wheel-drive vehicles as some of our opponents suggest.

Mountain bikers can serve their own cause by promoting an image of environmental consciousness. This can be done in a number of ways, limited only by the imagination. For example, they can take part in local Adopt a Trail programmes, in which civic groups agree to be responsible for maintenance of specific trails.

At the very least riders should adopt and follow the commonsense objectives of the Mountain Bike Code of Conduct agreed by the Countryside Commission and the Sports Council. Its advice on rights of way is that cyclists can ride on bridleways and byways but have no right to cycle on footpaths. On open land, such as moorland and farmland there is no right of access without express permission of the landowner. On canal towpaths cycling is allowed provided you have a permit from the British Waterways Board. Cycling on pavements is against the law. At all times cyclists should adhere to the Highway Code and the Country Code. Its salient points for mountain bikers are:

❑ Take care to fasten all gates
❑ Take your litter home
❑ Protect wildlife, plants and trees
❑ Take special care on country roads
❑ Keep to rights of way across farmland
❑ Leave livestock, crops and machinery alone
❑ Use gates and stiles to cross fences, hedges and walls
❑ Guard against all risks of fire
❑ Help to keep all water clean
❑ Make no unnecessary noise

## The Wonder of It All

When I was a small child, my father would take me and my siblings on what we called 'nature walks'. While he was no more informed in the field of biology than any other well-read layman, he taught us to observe without disturbing. For example, when we spotted an ant-hill, we at first wanted to tear it up, but he taught us to sit and observe the behaviour of the ants as they went about their ordinary business.

My mountain bike has permitted me to extend my range of such observations of nature, and I can say without hesitation that much of the grandeur I have seen and the natural wonders I have had the good fortune to appreciate would not have been part of my life had my bicycle not taken me to remote areas.

While some arch-conservationists have suggested that the cyclist is in too much of a hurry to take in and appreciate his surroundings, my experience refutes that position. By this standard, jogging or running in wild areas could be considered reprehensible! I don't feel that my appreciation of magnificent surroundings is diminished by the fact that I got there on a bicycle; the mountain bike is no more or less a tool of exploration than a pair of sturdy boots, except that it has a vastly increased range.

In some cases the bicycle is a more benign form of travel than more traditional forms, i.e. horses, yet the bicycle is legislated out of areas where the use of horses is a far more destructive element. Some years back I rode in an area that is now closed to bicycles, and on the trail I met a man leading a string of six pack-horses. One man, six horses; I wasn't under the impression that this man was repairing the obvious damage his livestock was causing, yet such use is still permitted where bikes are outlawed.

There is to date little scientific information regarding the environmental impact of mountain bikes, although a number of research projects are taking shape. In the next few years we can expect a wealth of data, but it is unlikely that the quoting of facts and figures will solve problems that are as much the result of emotional reactions as they are reasoned analyses.

We are all ambassadors for our sport every time we enter areas used by other afficionados of the outdoors. I ride as though the impression I create when I meet a hiker or an equestrian will be the only one he or she has of mountain bikers in general. The attitude is not universal among mountain bikers, but our cause would be well served if it were.

# The Future: 2003

The sport of mountain biking has grown phenomenally since 1976. By extending some of the trends that have established themselves, perhaps we can determine something of the future of our sport. Here are some imaginative examples of mountain bike news of the future.

## Chamonix, France, August 4, 2003

Approval was given today for the use of Mont Blanc as the site of the European Mountain Bike Downhill Championships. The course descends a little more than 7,000 feet in three-eighths of a mile, with one steep pitch where it drops 1,000 feet in a horizontal distance of 4 feet, a 25,000 per cent slope. Riders are said to be using specially modified bikes for the championships, with extra-fat tyres of very gummy rubber that last through only one or two runs down the course. Bikes have shock absorbers, and the riders wear G-suits so they can retain consciousness through some of the dips. 'That pullout at the bottom of "Ol' Hairball" is pretty rough,' says designer Brian Skinner, 'And these riders don't like to lose consciousness for even a fraction of a second. At practice speeds of around 110 mph you can crash pretty bad. At racing speeds you could hurt yourself.' Not to mention leaving an unsightly gouge in the course.

## Cuzco, Peru, January 3, 2009

Leader Arnold Jones of the Tierra Del Fuego-to-Point Barrow Mountain Bike Race passed through town today, maintaining his two-week lead over second place Pro-Am rider Elton Walters. The two broke away together from the rest of the pro pack early in the race, and had built a lead of as much as three weeks. They were within a day of each other as far as northern Argentina until Walters was robbed of his bike by bandits. Under World Mountain Bike Association (WOMBAT) rules, riders must be self-sustaining, and since he was 200 miles from his next money drop, Walters was forced to work as a waiter for two weeks until he had saved the money for a pistol, whereupon he took his bike back and continued in the race. Although it cost him his chance for the lead, it is classic stories such as this illustrating the resourcefulness, courage, and spirit on the part of the riders that make cross-continental mountain bike racing the colourful if somewhat unknown sport that it is.

Walters was philosophical about the delay. 'Those are the breaks, but there's a lot of racing left between here and Alaska. I figure I can make a move somewhere around northern Mexico, and if that doesn't work, I know Jones has always been weak in Idaho. And remember, it ain't over 'til it's over. Remember Ace Mitchell ten years ago? Ace was leading by a week going across Alaska. He'd just outridden that big avalanche that blocked the Yukon route for everyone else and was easing up a bit when he went and got eaten by a bear. All they found was some of his clothes, a lot of blood and his chain chewed to little bits. That's how they figured it was a bear— them critters just love the taste of oil, especially the new synthetic polyviscose chain-wheel LPX.'

Caught in a garrulous moment because he hadn't seen an English-speaking person in weeks, Walters enlightened reporters on other aspects of the race:

His course record of two years, one month, six days, four hours, eight minutes, 12.44 seconds: 'Jones is going well, but he's several hours off my record pace. The time I set the record I had everything on my side. My bike worked beautifully, I only had 63 flats, and I don't think I missed more than a couple of shifts.'

Pro-Am racing: 'This is my third Pro-Am, and I'm glad to get out of the other classes. Before turning pro I raced in the eighteen-to-eighteen-and-a-half-year-old, 144-pound, red-headed class. Some of those races are blood-baths, because no-one knows how to ride. I like the longer pro races, too. The longest off-road race for the novices and sport classes is only 3,000 miles and at best only 250,000 feet vertical, and I like the increased challenge of the pro distance.'

Diet for hopeful racers: 'Eat as much as you can as often as you can. Be prepared to live off road-kills or grass shoots. Know the 12 varieties of edible scorpions. In this kind of racing you are responsible for your own support, and unprepared riders can ''bonk out'', or run out of energy two or three days from a grocery store. In my first race I bonked and spent a week crawling across the Mexican desert. You'd better believe I never get on the bike anymore without making sure I have 50 or 60 pounds of food and a couple of gallons of water.'

The prize list: 'Pro Cross-Continental racing isn't the biggest part of the off-road scene, so the prize lists aren't as big as for some of the other races. I think the winner here gets 150 bucks, but it's kind of a matter of pride. My sponsor, Mega Bicycles— that's their logo tattooed on my knuckles—takes care of me with a salary that will add up to a couple of thousand dollars at the end of the race, with an incentive clause that says I have to finish to collect, and I get five bucks a day in expenses. Plus I get a free bike and two jerseys.'

How racing affects his marriage: 'I can't deny that it's tough for my wife when I race, but when I'm training between races I'm generally not gone for more than a week or two, a month maximum.'

# New Orleans, January 9, 2008

The Superdome was the site of the U.S. Indoor Mountain Bike Championships today, and rider Leroy 'Scuse My Dust' Baker was the winner after 122 laps of the 3/32 mile banked oval. Because of spectator seating on the field, which produced a record crowd of 133,000 for a mountain bike event, the course was the shortest yet used in national competition. The speed of the riders on the short course inspired promoters to bank the entire oval, with the ends significantly steeper. The dirt that was to be the original surface wouldn't handle the increased steepness, so a smooth surface of wooden planks was substituted. In order to thoroughly capture the spirit of mountain biking, dirt was sprinkled on the infield, and a number of potted plants were scattered throughout the auditorium, strategically located so as not to interrupt the view.

Riders responded to the fast course conditions with a number of interesting modifications to their equipment. Winner Leroy Baker used a 1-speed mountain bike with thinner tyres than usual, as well as the drop-style handlebars that were once popular on '10-speeds'. 'These tyres have a cross-section of only an inch, and no tread,' he explains. 'I pump them up to about 140 psi for a course like this, and I really fly. On a fast course the drop bars keep me in a more aerodynamic position. My wheels are aerodynamic discs without spokes, which you don't see too often at mountain bike races, but that helps when you're doing 40 mph.' Baker's bike has no brakes, and he explains that his 1-speed mountain bike uses a 'fixed' gear which he can back-pedal to slow down. 'On a course like this, without any serious downhills, brakes just get in the way.' The frame is made of exotic and expensive materials and the complete bike weighs about 12 pounds, which is considered light for a mountain bike. It is rumoured to have cost $14,000.

The race was close for the first 100 laps, as the riders bunched into a tight group. The group broke up when Baker's teammate 'Spokes' Higgins had a flat and stopped to fix it as required by race rules. Although team tactics are discouraged in mountain bike racing, Higgins managed to get in the way of all riders except Baker during the 16 laps it took for him to fix the tyre.

Mega Bicycles sponsored the event, and afterward a spokesman said that the latest event was the '. . . biggest mountain bike event ever. Over 100,000 people enjoyed mountain biking today in person, and millions more enjoyed it on television. A recent survey indicated that 62 million people in this country enjoy mountain biking, and of that number six million enjoy it so much that they even have bikes. And enjoyment is what mountain biking is all about.'

## Crested Butte, Colorado, September 28, 2010

The 35th Annual Pearl Pass Mountain Bike Tour is over, another successful promotion. From a group of as few as 13 on the 1978 tour, the event has grown to be a major stop on the mountain bike calendar, this year hosting nearly 23,000 riders.

The logistics of shepherding this huge group on the Tour might be a problem too complex for the most powerful computer, but the imaginative promoters have found a way to keep the impact to a minimum. The starting point of the tour has been moved from Elk Avenue in Crested Butte to downtown Denver, where the helpful police department blocks off a half-mile of Colfax Avenue. Instead of following the traditional route up Brush Creek, the Tour heads north on I-25, where a lane is blocked off, to the Boulder turn off. From there it's a short ride into Boulder. Two buses and a flatbed truck provide sag support for the inevitable stragglers and casualties in order to clear the highway within two hours as required by the permit.

The group is too large for the original camp site of the two-day tour, so riders 'camp' in Boulder's fine motels or on the campus of the University of Colorado. Riders who have paid for the luxury tour package are bussed from Boulder back to Denver for an evening of shopping, dinner, and dancing before setting up 'camp' at the luxurious Executive Towers downtown hotel. In the morning they are bused back to Boulder for the triumphant ride back into Denver, where riders disperse to several hundred local bars to laugh about their adventures over a beer or two.

Those interested in attending the Annual Pearl Pass Tour should contact Mega Bicycles of New York City. Packages range from the 'Bare Bones' at $198 to the luxury package at $1400 (double occupancy). A spokesman for Mega Bicycles announced that plans were in the works for next year's Pearl Pass Tour to take place simultaneously in New York, Los Angeles, New Orleans, and Denver to accommodate the expected 39,000 riders.

## Washington, D.C., June 9, 2011

By a vote of eight to one the Supreme Court today upheld NORBA vs. Park and Rec, a ruling which found that mountain bikes could be excluded from all public lands except the little-bitty part between the pavement and the kerb, on streets running north and south. Dissenting was Justice Hugo Heartburn, who said the measure did not go far enough to remove the scourge of mountain bikes from the land.

# Bibliography

## Books

*All-Terrain Bicycling*
By Charles Coombs, 118 pages, Henry Holt & Company, 1987.
This is an introduction to all-terrain bikes for younger readers. Adult readers will find it oversimplified, but it covers the basics of choosing and maintaining a bike. Safety on the bike is a major emphasis.

*All-Terrain Bikes*
By various authors, 92 pages, Rodale Press, 1985.
This book is a compendium drawn from articles on mountain bikes that have appeared in *Bicycling Magazine* (USA) since 1979. In spite of the fact that I contributed several of the articles that were used, this book is a relatively weak attempt to cash in on a growing market.

*The Bicycle and the Bush*
By Jim Fitzpatrick, 256 pages, Oxford University Press, 1980.
Mountain biking before mountain bikes were invented—a history of the safety bicycle in the Australian outback, where it was quickly and widely adopted in the 1890s as a form of transport, because 'it required no food or water, was two or three times as fast as a horse or camel, and did not drop dead from eating poisonous plants.' Many interesting photos and illustrations.

*Bicycles Up Kilimanjaro*
By Richard and Nicholas Crane, 154 pages, The Oxford Illustrated Press, 1985.
This lavishly illustrated book is an account of the Crane cousins' mountain bike expedition to the top of Africa's highest peak. Although they carried their bikes much of the distance, they did actually ride at the top nearly 20,000 feet above sea level. Profits from the book go to a charity, Intermediate Technology.

*Eugene Sloane's Complete Book of All-Terrain Bicycles*
By Eugene Sloane, 275 pages, Simon & Schuster, 1985.
Eugene Sloane wrote an enormously popular book on bicycles some years back, *Eugene Sloane's Complete Book of Bicycling*. The newer work is an attempt to duplicate the comprehensive nature in a book for mountain bikers, and although Sloane cannot be described as a pioneer in this field, he conducted extensive interviews and collected an impressive pile of equipment in writing this book. This work suffers a little from its dependence on specific brands as illustrations of the rapidly changing 'state of the art'.

*The Mountain Bike Book*
By Rob Van der Plas, 139 pages, Velo Press, 1984.
The first book to appear on the subject of mountain bikes, this work covers most of the basic 'how-to' aspects of repair and maintenance. Some of the historical references are a little distorted due to the fact that Mr. Van der Plas did most of his research far from the hotbeds of the sport, but basic repairs are treated in depth. Since *The Mountain Bike Book* appeared in 1984, a number of technical developments that have appeared since that time, principally the new braking systems, do not get a mention.

*The Mountain Bike Manual*
By Dennis Coello, 125 pages, Dream Garden Press, 1985.
This is a manual covering most of the basic questions asked by prospective bike purchasers. Since Mr. Coello's main experience has been in the realm of bicycle touring, this theme dominates the book. Because *The Mountain Bike Manual* concentrates on some of the specific brands of products in the rapidly evolving field, the book is somewhat dated, although most of the general information on repairs is useful.

*Wheels on Ice*
Edited by Terrance Cole, 64 pages, Alaska Northwest Publishing Company, 1985.
Not really a mountain bike book, *Wheels on Ice* deals with a related subject, cycling in Alaska during the Gold Rush between 1898 and 1908. Compiled from contemporary accounts and diaries, with many photos.

# Periodicals

Because mountain bikes are still evolving rapidly, periodical publications are a good way to keep up with the latest developments. Here is a selection of magazines and newsletters for mountain bikers. If you are interested in any of these, I suggest you send a self-addressed stamped envelope to them with a request for current subscription rates.

*Adventure Bike*
1727 Hamilton Street
Allentown, PA 18102
USA
This is a new quarterly tabloid publication, started in 1987, and to date has consisted of great photographs accompanied by shallow text.

*Bicycle Action*
136-38 New Cavendish Street
London W1M 7FG
England
The first UK magazine largely devoted to mountain bikes. It is now published by the people who market Muddy Fox bicycles.

*Bicycle Magazine*
The Northern and Shell Building
PO Box 381
Mill Harbour
London E14 9TW
England
Founded by Richard Ballantine, *Bicycle Magazine* was the first major English glossy colour bicycling magazine. Richard's connection with the publication ended in 1983, and it is now a mainstream bicycle magazine, with occasional articles on mountain biking.

*Bicycle Guide*
711 Boylston Street
Boston, MA 02116
USA
A mainstream bicycle magazine, with occasional articles on mountain biking.

*Bicycling*
33 East Minor Street
Emmaus, PA 18049
USA
A mainstream bicycle magazine, the largest U.S. cycling publication. Most issues include one or more mountain bike articles.

*Classic Bicycle and Whizzer News*
P.O. Box 765
Huntington Beach, CA 92648
USA
The CB&W News is produced sporadically by Leon Dixon, one of the foremost experts on old balloon-tyre bicycles. No mountain bikes here, in fact, few bikes made any more recently than the fifties. For collectors and afficionados of a classic era of American bicycles.

*Fat Tire Flyer*
My own publication and the source of some of the material in this book. Started in 1980, it is the original publication strictly for mountain bikers. Now sadly defunct.

*Freewheeling*
P.O. Box K26
Haymarket NSW 2000
Australia
A mainstream magazine for Australian cyclists, *Freewheeling* carries regular mountain bike features and a column for ATB riders called Fat Tyre Fanatic.

*Making Tracks*
55, Grafton Road
New Malden
Surrey KT3 3AA
England
A low-key publication for British mountain bikers, reminiscent of *Fat Tire Flyer* in its early days. Excellent source of information on local rides and clubs in England.

*Mountain Bike Action*
Daisy/Hi-Torque Publishing Company
10600 Sepulveda Boulevard
Mission Hills, CA 91345
USA
This is published by a company that has traditionally specialized in motorcycle and BMX publications, and as such deals primarily with the 'radical' aspects of mountain bike riding and racing.

*Mountain Bike for the Adventure*
Rodale Press
33 East Minor Street, Emmaus, PA 18049
USA
The second publication for mountain bikers to hit the market, this magazine was started in Colorado, one of the most active mountain bike areas. Emphasis is on mountain bike touring and the outdoor experience. If you liked what you've read so far, read this. I just joined as editor after *Fat Tire Flyer* folded.

*Mountain Bike Rider*
P.O. Box 12121
St. Paul, MN 55172
USA
A regional quarterly for riders in the northern Midwest.

*Mountain Biking*
Challenge Publications
7950 Deering Avenue
Canoga Park, CA 91304
USA
This is one of the newer publications, produced by an outfit that puts out special interest publications in several fields.

*Mountain Biking*
The Mountain Bike Club
3, The Shrubbery, Albert Street
St. Georges, Telford
Shropshire TF2 9AS
England
Newsletter of the English version of NORBA, with useful info on rides and events, and occasional technical articles and equipment test reports.

*New Cyclist*
14, St. Clement's Grove
York YO2 1JZ
England
New, committed, low-key quarterly aiming for in-depth editorial content in place of colour photos and regurgitated manufacturer's hand-outs. Outspoken contributors work for free. Occasional articles on mountain bikes.

*NORBA News*
Competition Publications
P.O. Box 1901
Chandler, AZ 85244
USA
The monthly newsletter of the National Off-Road Bicycle Association, with coverage of NORBA-sanctioned competition, including comprehensive lists of results. Sent to members of NORBA and distributed free through participating bicycle shops.

*Northeast ATB News*
P.O. Box 328
Roosevelt, NJ 08555
USA
A quarterly newsletter for riders in the Northeast U.S.

*Observed Trials Pedal'r*
P.O. Box 76
Beaumont, KS 67012
USA
The *Pedal'r* is aimed strictly at the new breed of bicycle Observed Trials rider, and is actually published by a company that makes trials bikes. A good source of information on who's who and where the action is in Observed Trials.

*Topanga Riders' Bulletin*
1582 Pride Street
Simi Valley, CA 93065
USA
Victor Vincente of America's outrageous contribution to immortal literature, this is truly one of the original mountain bike publications. Not for the faint of heart.

*Winning*
1727 Hamilton Street
Allentown, PA 18102
USA
A publication dealing strictly with bicycle racing, *Winning* is primarily for those interested in road racing, but from time to time the US edition covers the more important events and personalities in off-road competition. There is also a UK edition.

# Organizations

Association Quebecoise du Velo de Montagne
C.P. 425, Haute-Ville Quebec
Quebec G1R 4R5
Canada
This association sanctions and promotes mountain bike events in eastern Canada, primarily the province of Quebec.

The Mountain Bike Club (National Off-Road Bicycle Association U.K.)
3, The Shrubbery
Albert Street, St. Georges
Telford, Shropshire
England
The English version of NORBA is a club which provides insurance for races and other events as well as coordinating national and international mountain bike activities affecting British riders. Members receive subscriptions to a newsletter, *Mountain Biking*.

Mountain Bikers of Alaska
2900 Boniface Parkway
Suite 657
Anchorage, AK 99504
USA
The MBA organize and promote the incredible Iditabike Challenge, a 200-mile mountain bike race/trek in the snow on the legendary Iditarod Trail.

The National Off-Road Bicycle Association (U.S.)
P.O. Box 1901
Chandler, AZ 85244
USA
Commonly abbreviated as NORBA, this privately owned company sanctions and insures most of the mountain bike racing in the United States, as well as promoting National Championship events. Started in 1983 as a non-profit association, NORBA was turned over to private ownership later that year, and is now owned by the American Bicycle Association, a BMX sanctioning and promoting company.

NORBA Canada
810 East 12th Avenue
Vancouver, BC V5T 2J2
Canada
A non-profit society sanctioning most of the racing in the western part of Canada, primarily the West Coast. Members receive their own newsletter, the *Knobby News*.

**Nick Crane**

## PART TWO: EXPEDITIONS
### Nick Crane

**Trans-Sahara 1982-83**

# The Perfect Expedition Machine

**E**xpeditions are normally regarded as the preserve of men with thick beards who tramp stoically at the head of columns of porters bearing all the impedimentia associated with grant-aided holidays—sorry—scientific research programs. But there are other expeditions, too: the sort that anyone can try: low cost, independent adventures.

Definition: An expedition is a journey which seems to take more time to organize than to execute. An 'expedition' can last a day or a year. An expedition is difficult, there is an element of the unknown (and therefore a challenge to both courage and knowledge) and its success depends on a level of planning not usually needed for a casual excursion. A cycling expedition could be an attempt to cross a mountainous area or to get from A to B off-road in a day. Or it could be a circular ride through a navigationally tricky wilderness of forest and moor. At the ambitious end of the scale a cycling expedition could lead you across deserts and high plateaux; through sandstorms or thin air.

It is interesting to note just how quickly the bicycle took off as an expedition vehicle. Not more than 15 years separated the invention of the tensioned wheel and the pushing off in 1884 from San Francisco of the original bike hero Thomas Stevens, aboard his 50-inch Columbia Expert. Stevens became the first man to cycle around the world.

History's instant recognition of the bicycle as an expedition vehicle has always reinforced my view that this lightweight, self-propelled, energy-efficient, pollution-free method of long distance travel will never be superseded. Compare for example the bicycle and the roller-skate. The roller-skate was invented much earlier than the bicycle, by a Belgian called Jean Joseph Merlin, in 1760. The fact that the first roller-skate expedition (Theodore Coombs's marathon skate from Los Angeles to New York and down to Kansas) did not take place until 1979—two centuries after its invention—indicates a certain reluctance on the part of overland travellers to adopt it as an expedition vehicle. I mean this as no slur on roller-skaters. It is just that a vehicle capable of carrying ten times its own weight; that runs 1,000 miles (1,600 kilometers) on a thimbleful of oil; that can cross continents in a matter of days; that can handle roads or riverbeds, Himalayan passes or the Nubian Desert, is not just clean, quick and cheap, but *very* versatile.

Of course it would be unfair to mention Thomas Stevens without noting some others from the expeditioneers' hall of fame. While Stevens was away on his 3-year penny-farthing ride, the 'Safety' bicycle was invented. With two wheels of the same size, pneumatic tyres, and gears, the Safety quickly took over the roads of Europe and America. The first big ride on Safety's started in 1896, when John Foster Fraser, S. Edward Lunn, and F.H. Lowe rode across 17 countries and 3 continents, notching up 19,237 miles (30,952 kilometers) mostly on dirt roads. It was the longest bike ride to date. The next hundred years are busy with bike expeditions. One thinks of Bernard Newman (60 countries and 100 books about cycling), Jesse Hart Rosdail (11,626 miles (18,706 kilometers) on a £5 three-speed), Louise Sutherland (round the world on a secondhand *one*-speed), Walter Stolle (159 countries and 402,000 miles (646,818 kilometers), Harold Elvin (30 countries on a 3-speed), Dervla Murphy (Ireland to India on a 37 lb. bike; 34 lb. of luggage), Ian Hibell (Alaska to Tierra del Fuego via the Darien Gap; North Cape of Norway to Cape Town via the Sahara Desert), Takafumi Ogasawara (round the world on a *folding* bicycle), Wiegand Horst Lichtenfels (47,500 miles (76,428 kilometers) on a bike and luggage totaling 400 pounds), Kojiro Hirayama (round the world; Hirayama was deaf and dumb), Wally Watts (10,000 miles (16,000 kilometers) and 16 countries on a *uni*-cycle).

If all this has already been done on a ramshackle flotilla of unicycles, junkyard specials, penny-farthings and shopping bikes, what is there left for a mountain bike? Well, there's more puncture-proof travelling for a start. Round-the-world traveller Ragubir Singh had to mend 410 during his 93,000-mile epic world tour. What would he have given for a mountain bike?

The first great mountain bike journey was Tim Gartside and Peter Murphy's crossing of the Sahara Desert in the early months of 1983. These two Australian lawyers covered 3,410 miles (5,487 kilometers) during their north-south crossing riding the first Japanese-built Tom Ritchey designed frames. Gartside and Murphy, who finished the trip in Niger, later returned to the UK where they were at the forefront of mountain bike activities (one as the main mover of mountain bike events; the other as editor of *Bicycle Action,* then the main mountain bike magazine) for the following few years.

As production mountain bikes started to arrive in Europe they were quickly taken up by the 'peak baggers'. The highest mountains in England, Scotland, and Wales were knocked off within weeks of mountain bikes arriving in Britain. Mountain bikes then went on to reach the summits of the highest mountains in Europe and Africa. The journey to the top of Kilimanjaro, Africa's highest mountain, is covered later in this book. The successful attempt on Mont Blanc, Europe's highest, was made by Jaap Lampe and Eric Pootjes, who rode and hauled their mountain bikes all the way to the top. The record for cycling at altitude is currently held by Adrian Crane (a cousin), who took a mountain bike to 20,561 feet (6,267 meters) on Mount Chimborazo in South America. Fuji has fallen, too. (It is interesting to note that volcanoes—Kilimanjaro, Fuji, Chimborazo—tend to offer better biking than mountains that have been ice-sculpted such as Mont Blanc; Lampe and Pootjes had to dismantle their bikes and use ropes during their climb.)

Everest has still to fall but in Tibet in 1986 seemed choc-a-bloc with mountain bikes (a slight exaggeration I know, but there were many of them about). Nonetheless lugging bikes to mountain summits has a limited future. Despite the arrival of mountain bikes it is still quicker and safer to travel on a mountain by foot; the peak bagging fad was born of an adrenalin surge sparked by first sight of knobby tires and raunchy handlebars. The real future of mountain bikes is along the rough byways of remote areas where bicycles (with horses and feet) are the most environmentally sympathetic forms of travel.

Before we explore the practicalities of expedition cycling, I have to admit to an antitechnical bias: unlike the pioneers like Breeze, Fisher, Ritchey, Kelly, and the rest of the ingenious crew, I belong to the school of opportunists for whom inventions are but a key to adventures which lie beyond. I've never felt the urge to shorten my top tube or experiment with radical rakes; and I've never pondered upon the physics that make a mountain bike as fleet of foot as a flying quarter horse—when I first saw a mountain bike, I just knew from the look of the thing that it would open doors to a world beyond the range of the traditional touring bike.

Bicycles of different shapes and sizes have taken me to 26 countries, on rides that have ranged from a haphazard caper across the Great African Rift Valley to a neatly planned circumnavigation of Europe's biggest ice-field. The bikes used have varied from single-speed roadsters to slick 10-speed tourers. I'm probably not alone in having been thwarted from time to time by the relative fragility of conventional bikes. A couple of instances spring to mind: once, I carried an aluminium folding Bickerton bicycle to the top of a Welsh mountain and attempted to ride it down . . . with predictably painful results (the small wheels were a perfect fit for rabbit holes). And on a rough crossing of the Picos de Europa range of mountains in northern Spain my normally trusty touring bike punctured at the height of a storm and minutes before dark on a remote shelterless plateau. Mountain bikes for me meant breaking clear of the kind of trip that is dictated by the mechanical limitations of the bike; mountain bikes meant I could go more or less where I pleased; they meant freedom.

So, pull on your pith helmet . . . .

# Software

## What Expedition?

You're looking for a challenge—mental and physical. It has got to be hard enough for the outcome to be uncertain, but not so hard that nobody will insure you. It's got to be fun. And it's got to be interesting. And ideally, it has not been done before. So, how do you go about designing an expedition?

Dreaming up a good goal—remember that an 'expedition' is a journey with a clear-cut objective—can be rather like trying to compose the perfect meal: there are millions of permutations but only *one* is going to fit the mood and taste of the day. Finding the perfect goal is a matter of exploring the possibilities. Let's imagine you've got the hunger. . . .

In the local library you find a reference to a Swiss pilot, Willi Unterkart, who in 1923 crashed his plane into a mountaintop while trying to find the remote and legendary 'grey' city of B'hambhingham-tsoola (in the original Dryptik tongue, B'hambhingham--tsoola roughly translates to Birmingham South but early romantic explorers preferred the more exotic sound of Bambazoola). The wreckage of the plane was discovered 30 years later by oil prospectors, but Unterkart—and the city—have never been found.

Eureka! A great idea! How about searching for the Great Grey City! By bike!

## Mountain Bikes to Bamabazoola!

The first thing to do after getting a great idea is to calm down. The second thing to do is to tell no one. Except your family, best friends, helpful friends . . . etc., etc.

There will be plenty of advice offered. Nearly all of it will be of the 'You'll never do it/The bikes will break' variety. The only people who offer positive advice are those that want to join the expedition.

# Attitude

The world's wildernesses are the last (shrinking) reminders we have of a life gone before. Beyond the itching frontiers of 'civilization' lies the index to Man's future. If we destroy it, we will no longer know where we come from or have the means to go forward. It is *so* precious; *so* totally irreplaceable and *so* crucial to our futures that travel through these places must be on tippy-toe, not clod-hopping boot. The days of 4 × 4 expeditions mashing nature underwheel are over.

And wilderness travel is not about 'survival' either; it's about understanding. Landscapes cannot 'threaten' us; it's the landscapes that keep us alive; we threaten ourselves. With the right attitude and equipment there is nowhere on the earth's surface that man cannot exist in comparative comfort.

# Planning

Since nobody is quite sure of the whereabouts of Bamboozala, buying the appropriate maps is going to be a bit of a problem. What we do know is that the first 1,000 kilometers of riding are going to be on charted roads. For this we need maps of two scales: about 1:1,000,000, which is handy for overview planning, and 1:200,000 (1 centimeter to 2 kilometers) for detailed route planning. Most countries have national surveys at 1:200,000 (and many have even larger scale maps at 1:50,000). Bamboozala, however, lies somewhere in the midst of an unpopulated mass of mountains and desert plateaux for which only satellite-mapping at 1:1,000,000 is available. Never mind. At least the main dirt roads will be shown on the map.

Having bought the maps, the next stage is to measure the total riding distance. Divide this by the number of miles (or kilometers) you expect to ride in one day. On dirt roads of unknown surfaces you should expect to average (allowing for, say, one day off the bike in every week) no more than 62 miles (100 kilometers) a day. There will be days when twice this average is possible; others when you would be hard pushed to cover half the average.

You now have the total time needed to ride to Bamboozala—or roughly where you think it might be. The next question is: 'What is the best time of year for the ride?' Here we are looking at temperature, and to a lesser extent winds and humidity. There may be other factors to consider too, such as mountain passes that do not clear of snow till late spring, or rivers swollen by spring thaws that tear away the bridges. Temperatures of below 32° Fahrenheit mean carrying extra clothing; temperatures above 90°F are seriously hot and will cause major dehydration and therefore require detailed attention to liquids.

On the road to Bamboozala there are additional complexities: in five places the roads reach altitudes of 16,400 feet (5,000 meters). Air temperature drops at approximately 1.8°F for every 490 feet (150 meters) climbed (in dry air the rate can be 1.8°F for every 328 feet (100 meters) of ascent, and in cloudy conditions a slower cooling of 1.8°F for every 656 feet (200 meters) of ascent—these are guide figures only and are liable to vary according to local conditions). Together with the cooling affect of increasing altitude, you must also consider the implications of windchill.

Windchill is particularly significant for cyclists because when we reach the top of a long pass, I, at least, am normally so hot that I have steam coming out of my ears. To freewheel straight down the other side without wrapping up in layers of insulating clothing and windproofs is foolhardy and dangerous. The rush of cold air freezes exposed flesh and penetrates clothing; very quickly your muscles seize up, your body core temperature plummets, and before you know what is happening you're shivering so violently you can hardly balance the bike. Windchill is most marked at the speeds that cyclists experience when travelling fast: freewheeling at 30 mph (50 kph) down a mountain pass, whose still air temperature is 35°F, will produce a numbing windchill factor of 6°F.

So you can see that together, altitude and windchill can have a serious affect on your body temperature unless you anticipate the changes and alter your clothing accordingly. On a practical point: pulling on gloves, a warm hat (which covers the ears), protection for the neck, and a windproof layer for the chest will dramatically slow the rate of windchill cooling. Racing cyclists often stuff a newspaper up the front of their jerseys as they crest a mountain col and begin their descent.

On passes and plateaux of over 6,500 feet (2,000 meters) we must also prepare for the effects of thinning air, which makes the breathing laboured and in extreme cases leads to dehydration and altitude sickness. The effect of altitude varies from person to person; some people can pedal up to 9,800 feet (3,000 meters) without noticing; others will be huffing and puffing sooner. At heights of 9,800-16,400 feet (3,000-5,000 meters) the shortage of oxygen has an increasingly dramatic effect on a cyclist's performance. The way round this is to acclimatize gradually; if your ride includes 16,400-foot passes, you will need several days at an altitude of between 6,500 and 13,000 feet (2,000 and 4,000 meters) before it is safe to go higher. The mountaineer's maxim 'work high, sleep low' is worth remembering; the effect of altitude can be lessened if you plan your itinerary so that you sleep as low as possible. It is also essential to increase your intake of liquids when cycling high. You soon find that cycling the giant passes is rather like climbing a mountain; each pass has to be regarded as an expedition in itself, with a planned time to reach the top, allowances made for clothing stops, a definite idea of where the points of shelter are likely to be (in the event of sudden storms or impossible winds) and enough liquid to see you through to the next water source.

Still on the maps, the next stage is to discover how many people live in the areas along the route, and how much traffic uses the road. Armed with these two bits of information it will be possible to hypothesize on the regularity of roadside villages, and therefore of local stores which sell food. (Bear in mind that in many parts of the world where there are no shops, local people are often willing to exchange surplus domestic food for much needed currency). If you are food-faddish and are averse to trying exotic local dishes you have no alternative but to bring supplies of home-produced dehydrated muck. Carrying the extra weight will slow you down.

The other factor that will affect your luggage is whether you plan to use local accommodation or to be self-contained with a tent and its associated paraphernalia. Camping has the advantage that each day can be molded according to your energies: you can put up the tent when you feel the day has naturally run its course. The disadvantage is the extra weight of the hardware (see below). In favour of local accommodation is the extra fun you get from mixing with new people each night; overnight kit can be limited to a sleeping bag and you can nearly always eat where you sleep. The only disadvantage is that each day's ride has to fit available accommodation stops (it is always worth asking villagers where the nearest inn is; often the smallest of places can sustain a travellers' halt).

## Making Tracks

There are some obvious rules for starting out on an expedition:

● Ease into the miles gently; initially set daily targets two-thirds of your expected average, to allow for gear adjustments, acclimatizing, and getting fit.

● Use the first few days to (critically) re-evaluate your equipment and bike. If there is gear you don't need, dump it or post it home; if there are bits and pieces you hadn't thought of (such as face masks for the dust, or a hat with a peak) buy them locally before you leave the built-up areas.

● If you are riding with a companion, make sure to use these early days to iron out areas of dissention and conflict, so that you know exactly where you stand when the going gets tough.

Once you're riding, the three essential elements to watch are: direction, time and weather.

Navigation in Bamboozala is going to be fun. Your satellite map doesn't mark any villages and seems to have overlooked most of the minor roads. Normally it is not until you've been on the road for a few days that you begin to 'feel' your way into a landscape and the idiosyncracies of its route marking. Learning the relationship between your maps, the signposts, and what the landscape actually looks like, can be picked up quickly enough. A compass is often helpful at confusing junctions. You should never set off down a dirt track in wild country without being aware of its general compass direction. If you are relying on local villages for water, you cannot afford to get lost. Side tracks may go in circles or just disappear into the dust, or run to abandoned mine workings.

So a compass (and of course the knowledge and confidence to use it accurately) is vital for expedition cycling. Backup navigation can be achieved using a watch and the direction of the sun, or at night in the Northern Hemisphere by searching out the Pole Star. In clear weather the sun is a good rough guide to direction.

Time may be important because the country you're in may become too hot for riding during the middle of the day. When you know you are going to be forced into the shade for three or four hours during the middle of the day, rise before dawn, eat and get on the bike at first light. In India I've managed to get in as much as 62 miles (100 kilometers) before stopping for breakfast. After the heat, in late afternoon, you can resume the ride and continue until the cool of nightfall. The other reason for watching the clock is the need to reach shelter before dark. Whether you are putting up a tent or searching a Tibetan town for lodgings, it becomes a hundred times harder in the dark.

There are few places in the world that have entirely predictable weather. Deserts may be hot and sunny, but sandstorms of staggering intensity can appear from nowhere and blow for days; equatorial areas can be crisp and clear one moment, battered beneath a monsoon onslaught the next. Suspicious looking clouds and sudden unexpected gusts of wind often presage a violent change of climatic mood. Often you have to make a snap decision whether to dive for cover or ride it out. Nearly always the former is more prudent: once you have got soaking wet or reduced to an exhausted sand-blinded wreck, it is too late. From shelter you can observe the problem and coolly decide what to do next.

# Overnighting

Successful overnighting is part art, part science. First, camping. You've got the lightweight tent and cooking gear. The road to Bamboozala passes through huge areas of deserted scrubland. Campsites are two-a-penny. Or are they?

I'm a firm believer in the school of thought that opts for inconspicuous camping. If a tent is out of sight, it won't attract the attention of curious passers by, and provided the ground is left exactly as you found it you may as well have been a spirit in the night. The best tent pitches are out of sight, out of the wind and on level ground. Good places include hollows (provided they are well drained), the lee side of woods, and raised river terraces. In steep, mountainous areas it can often be difficult to find a patch of level ground large enough to take a tent. Places to look include the top of the promontory of land that forms the inside of a hairpin bend, and the land immediately adjacent to cols (these pitches are usually exposed and windy). And of course it is always possible to ask a farmer whether you can put up the tent on his land.

Camping without a tent is an overnight mode of which I'm particularly fond. With nothing more than a sleeping bag and groundsheet you have even more freedom than you have with a tent. Once your eye can focus on the nooks and crannies of a land-scape, there seems to be literally thousands of beds in every view. Again, you are looking for sheltered corners, and in areas of temperate climate you need a contingency plan for nighttime rain. Some groundsheets can keep off a modest drizzle; in more persistent rain you may have to saddle up and ride for cover. As I'm riding I often play an idle game: scouring the passing landscape for good campsites. It trains the eye.

The indoor accommodation option is great fun if you're gregarious by nature. Each night can bring a festival of entertainment as you sample even weirder rest halts than the night before. In areas of high population (such as southern Asia) there are hotels in most big villages and so the choice is wonderful. Most often it is possible to take the bike into the hotel room. The advantage of sleeping indoors is that your evenings are spared for sampling the local colour, trying exotic foods, and making friends. In remote areas, the arrival of foreign cyclists normally encourages a massive turn-out of spectators.

# Software Checklist

These, then, are the points you should have considered before setting off on a mountain bike expedition:

## The objective and the timing

You know exactly what your objective is, have estimated how long it will take to reach and return, and have chosen the best season for making the ride.

## Permissions

You have obtained the necessary permits/visas and so on for the journey.

## Insurance

You have insured your bike and equipment, and yourself (policy to include air repatriation). Check the small print because many insurance companies will baulk when it comes to bicycling to somewhere like Bambazoola.

## Information

You have researched your objective thoroughly, using maps, books from the local library, and first hand information from travellers who have already been thataway (note that travellers have a habit of exaggeration; moderately harmless episodes can transform into hair-raising life-and-death dramas in the telling of a tale).

## Maps

You have obtained the best maps for the ride, and extracted vital route information and sightseeing data which you will carry with you.

## Skills

You have practised before leaving home all the basic skills such as tent erection in the dark (if you have a tent), building emergency shelters, navigation, effecting quick bike repairs such as a broken chain, gear cables, derailleurs, spokes and basic maintenance such as adjusting hub bearings and removing shims from freewheels (if shims are fitted).

## Emergencies

You have made contingency plans should you be injured, lose all your money or equipment, or be turned back at a border. If you are travelling with a companion or in a team, you have discussed emergency procedures so that you all respond predictably should the need arise—or if an emergency happens while you are separated.

## Medical

You have consulted your own doctor (and perhaps specialist tropical doctors, too) and are aware of all the possible ailments from which you might suffer; you are acquainted with the appropriate preventive measures and remedies.

## Money

You have a budget, based on travel costs (flights etc.,) plus daily living costs plus 'red tape' charges (unforeseen permits etc.) plus extra for emergencies,

## Fitness

You have achieved a level of fitness that will allow you to quickly acclimatize; being physically fit will also ease the mental pressure of the first few days of the expedition.

# Useful Reading

This is by no means an exhaustive list ...

Ballantine, Richard. *Richard's New Bicycle Book* (Oxford Illustrated Press, Sparkford, 1988).

Crane, Nicholas. *The Great Bicycle Adventure* (Oxford Illustrated Press, Sparkford, 1987).

Crane, Nicholas and Crane, Richard. *Bicycles up Kilimanjaro* (Oxford Illustrated Press, Sparkford, 1985).

Crane, Richard and Crane, Nicholas. *Journey to the Center of the Earth* (Bantam Press, London, 1987).

Fraser, John Foster. *Round the World on a Wheel* (Chatto & Windus, London, 1982) (reprint).

Langmuir, Eric. *Mountaincraft and Leadership* (The Scottish Sports Council, Edinburgh, 1984).

Shales, Melissa (ed.). *The Traveler's Handbook* (Wexas Ltd, London, 1988).

Stevens, Thomas. *Around the World on a Bicycle* (Century Hutchinson, London, 1988) (edited reprint).

# Hardware

## The Bike

Do not get misled by the belief that you *have* to own the whizziest mountain bike in the world in order to embark upon an expedition. Some of my most enjoyable adventures have been on bikes most people wouldn't trust for a trip to the shops.

There are three types of bike that can be used for an expedition: the take-it-or-leave-it cheap heap; the off-the-peg production bike, and the not-a-penny-spared superbike. Over the years I have tried all three and quite a number of in-betweens.

The heap is well suited to the rider in no hurry and with flexible goals. I used one to cycle across the Great African Rift Valley with my cousin Adrian. It was the kind of ride for which mountain bikes were built. Unfortunately they hadn't quite been invented. Nearly the whole route was on rough roads, the worst of which consisted of deep ruts filled to the brim with bulldust. I had an ancient Philips roadster that fell apart by the mile until cracked forks, a snapped pedal spindle, and a disintegrated freewheel rendered it completely unridable. It didn't matter, because part of the fun of *that* particular expedition was in 'making do'. On the end of a length of rope, Adrian towed me and the crippled Philips into the nearest town, where we found a welder who quickly rebuilt the bike and sent us on our way.

The modern equivalent of that Philips is the kind of mountain bike you can pick up for a few pounds and which is clearly going to break at some time in your journey. If you cannot afford anything better, it is still going to be a lot of fun. I'm not *recommending* setting off on a trip with dubious machinery; just illustrating that the world won't necessarily end if the bike suffers apparently catastrophic breakdowns.

The second sort of bike is the standard middle-range production mountain bike. The advantage of this modest beast is that by making a few inexpensive modifications you can create a bike capable of tackling the toughest terrain. The mountain bikes cousin Richard and I took up Kilimanjaro started life as unexciting Saracens. They had enormously long wheelbases, and by today's standards handled like slugs on the uphills. But they were sufficient: the Mitsubishi Canyon Express tyres had a tread pattern that could cope equally well with sticky mud, lava gravel, and compacted snow, while the transmission may not have been state-of-the-art but it worked and didn't break. Before we set off up the mountain we took the two bikes north from Nairobi for a workout. A test ride down the slopes of the Rift Valley showed up a couple of areas for improvement: the gears were not low enough, so we fitted bigger sprockets to give a bottom gear of 19.2 inches, and we managed to snap a chain. Neither bike gave us any problems during the ascents and descent of the mountain; we didn't even manage to record any punctures!

The final type of mountain bike for expedition work is the fantasy-hybrid that is designed as a one-off to suit a particular expedition. For 'Journey to the Centre of the Earth'—reaching a remote point in Central Asia that was the place on earth furthest from any ocean—we had built for us two machines, the stuff of which dreams are made. Raleigh's chief designer Gerald O'Donovan had set out to produce for us two unique 'sprint' mountain bikes. We were looking for machines that could be ridden hard over surfaces varying from Himalayan snow and Tibetan stones to the sands and gravels of the Gobi desert. So we needed the tyre grip and balance of a mountain bike. And since our route would take us across the biggest plateau in the world, where thin air and many mountain passes would mean that we would need every calorie of energy we could muster, the bikes would have to be ultra-lightweight, too. Our final demand was that the bikes be fast, for to reach the 'Centre of the Earth' before the desert became unbearably hot, we would have to be pushing 93 miles (150 kilometers) a day. What we were asking for was a cross between a mountain bike, a road racing bike, and a touring bike.

We started with the wheels. Tim Gartside (who with Peter Murphy had made the first trans-Sahara mountain bike ride in 1982) had already been experimenting with lightweight wheels in his search for the ultimate racing mountain bike. After some experimentation he had come up with a combination of Mavic M3CD rims, Campagnolo hubs, and pre-stretched stainless steel spokes. After running these on his new Midnight Express machine, he recommended that we use them for our ride to the heart of Asia. The M3CD rims had the great advantage that a number of tyre sizes could be used on them; we planned to start the ride on 1¼-inch Specialized Touring K4's, then switch to 1⅜-inch Specialized Expeditions when the roads got rougher.

Reynolds 753 tubes silver-soldered to a geometry based on the bikes used by the Raleigh professionals in the murderous Paris-Roubaix classic race formed a frame that was both featherweight and incredibly strong. Gerald built the frame with extra clearances on the forks and stays to allow space for the chunky tyres. Following another mountain bike law, Gerald also built the frames an inch smaller than those we normally used for racing and touring. This would improve the bikes' handling on bouldery surfaces, gravel, and snow.

We settled for 10 speeds, with ratios ranging from 39 inches up to 95 inches, and to save weight we fitted a single gear lever. To change chainrings we could kick the chain down with our heel, or drag it up with a finger (this is not as mad as it sounds: on *major* rides where the passes are 16,400 feet (5,000 meters), you normally pause at the top to pull on windproof suits, so it is little extra effort to do a static gear change at the same time). We used standard Shimano 600 gears and chainsets. During the ride we managed to shed a few more grams from the bikes; in the sweltering Indian town of Siuri we borrowed a hacksaw and file, and cut our single gear lever in half to leave a 35mm stump. At the same time we sawed off the wheel guides from the brakes. Some of these amputations were for our own amusement: the psychological advantage to be gained in believing that you have the lightest bike possible is one of the little 'mind tricks' that can help the miles dissolve (if your bike is finessed to the final gram, it can no longer be a scapegoat for poor performance). It was all these minute reductions, in addition to removal of the chainset dustcaps, the ends of the toe straps and so on, that contributed to the low overall weight of the bikes: 22 lb.

Again, using mountain bike experience, we wanted wide handlebars. On the worst surfaces we would need our hands widely spaced to provide better balance and leverage, but on the faster sections of tarmac we would want to be using 'drops'. So we fitted the widest Cinelli square racing drops we could find. The brakes were Campagnolo side pulls fitted to Shimano Dura-Ace levers; we had Brooks Professional leather saddles.

At the end of 3,410 miles (5,500 kilometers) of desert and mountain, the bikes were in perfect working order. We suffered two punctures each, and a broken gear cable. The wheels were as true as they were when they left the hands of Bob Arnold in London's F.W. Evans.

Of course, it doesn't follow that the best bike guarantees a successful expedition. On one of my earlier mountain bike excursions, a night ride along the ancient Ridgeway, a chance branch caught in the wheel and turned the exotic SunTour derailleur inside out.

## Equipment and Clothing

On any expedition you are trying to achieve a balancing act between weight and safety (and to some extent, comfort). You need enough equipment 1) to protect you from the elements; 2) to keep the bike running; 3) to keep your body running.

Consider these advantages of a lightly loaded bike:
● it retains its agility on rough surfaces;
● a small amount of luggage is much easier to 'protect' than a large amount;
● a lightly-loaded bike can be lifted off the ground easily (useful for public transport, crossing landslides, mountain trails, flights of stairs to hotel bedrooms, etc.);
● a lightly loaded bike minimizes pedalling effort.

For lightweight travel in most parts of the world it is possible to keep total luggage weight (including clothes) under 20 pounds. This is about half what most cycletourists carry.

There are three areas where it is easy to overpack: camping gear, food, and comfort. If you are taking a tent and cooking gear (stove, fuel, pans, etc.) then it will be difficult to keep under the 20 lb. limit. If you are unwilling to rely on buying local foods then forget the weight and tow a trailer. And if perhaps you are considering taking an in-flatable bed and slippers, well . . . ! I'll admit to a fairly extreme view of the ideal luggage, and of course each of us has our own essential list of items to take. The golden rule is never to allow the quest for weight-saving to interfere with safety. Try wiping your mind of all the product advertising and start afresh by asking: 'What is the absolute minimum I need for this journey?'

# The Minima-List

## Clothes

● Shorts/jersey: Skin-fit, made from material which is both windproof and quick-drying. Or custom make some one-piece salopets, which save weight and avoid the 'cold gap' that can appear between shorts and jersey.

● Footwear: Cycling shoes with semi-stiffened soles if most of the route is going to be ridable; lightweight hiking boots with cleated soles if much bike carrying is envisaged.

● Underwear: Cotton is the most comfortable.

● Thermal underwear: Long johns and long-sleeved vest (vests with a high, zippered polo-neck provide essential insulation right up to the chin). Silk is the warmest and most comfortable, but also the most expensive.

● Shirt: T-shirt can be worn between thermal layer and cycling jersey, or next to the skin.

● Leg-warmers: Very versatile; can be pulled onto legs or arms, or used as a scarf.

● Jacket: Goretex, with front zipper for temperature control and with tough fitted hood, drawstringed to shelter face. Cuffs and waist should be snug fit to keep out the weather; bottom of jacket should overlap top of Goretex pants when leaning forward on bike. Jacket is about the most important garment; some jackets need extra seals down the front zipper to keep out driving rain or wind.

● Pants: Goretex, with Velcro tabs at ankles to prevent the bottoms flapping into the chain. Pants should be cut generously at hips and knees to allow unrestricted cycling.

● Thermal mitts: Mittens, with all four fingers sharing the same compartments, are warmer than gloves, which allow each finger to freeze individually. Mittens can also be pulled over feet in emergencies (gloves cannot!). Use mittens with a thermal fleece lining and windproof outer.

● Balaclava: Fibre-pile is very warm and dries quicker than wool. Balaclavas can be worn as total head-coverings, or folded to form a cap with a peak for use in bright sunlight.

**A nook for the night during the epic Journey to the Centre of the Earth**

● Goggles: Essential for high altitude cycling where the ultraviolet can damage eyes, and for dusty conditions (in deserts for example). Goggles with a 'nose-flap' and sidepieces shield the eyes from dust ingress.

## Sleeping

● Sleeping bag: Down bags with no zippers are the lightest; bags with a full-length zipper can be spread open and used as a blanket cover in hotter climates. Note that a sleeping bag can also perform as daytime clothing: by wrapping it around your body and then pulling on a Goretex jacket, you create a toasty-warm duvet-jacket. If the sleeping bag has a full length zipper, then the foot of the bag can be worn over your head, held in place by the hood of your jacket.
● Tents: If you are taking a tent, study the market carefully. Some of the double skin tents are now as light as Goretex 'bivvy bags',while being more comfortable and drier.

## General equipment

● Small knife: Useful for anything from adapting clothing to cutting cheese.
● Compass: The plastic, liquid-filled models are the best and the lightest.

● Watch: Save weight by cutting off the strap. A watch with 'hands' is quicker to use for sun navigation than a digital watch.

● Small spoon: This is all you need for eating. Five millitre plastic hospital spoons are the lightest.

● Needle: For mending clothes and dealing with blisters (sterilize needle in boiling water or in flame of match first).

## Bike equipment

● Panniers/backpack: If most of the riding is on roads and ridable tracks, carry your luggage in two small rear-mounted panniers. Most pannier systems have insufficiently strong mounting systems for prolonged off-road riding. A single nylon strap running from the bottom of one bag, up over the pannier rack, and down round the second bag, attached at both ends to the bottom of the rack, will grip both bags tightly and prevent bounce-offs on wild ground. Most panniers have a superfluity of zippers and buckles, which can be cut off. For prolonged off-road riding where the terrain is so difficult that panniers will catch on rocks or scrub, or will upset the handling of the rear end of the bike, it is better to carry luggage (15 lb. maximum) in a backpack. This is only satisfactory for short, concentrated bursts of riding over very rough terrain; wearing a backpack for road or trail riding is tiring.

● Pannier racks: Aluminium models with the triangulated geometry are the lightest and most stable.

● Containers: A bottle cage fitted to the down tube can be used for carrying ½-litre or 1-litre drinking bottles. A cage beneath the down tube (just forward of the bottom bracket) can be used for carrying a plastic pot filled with heavy items such as tools or film. The pot also doubles up as an eating/drinking vessel.

## Bike tools

● Pump: Frame fit for road and trail riding, or a short pump carried in the backpack for serious off-road riding where the bike has to be carried frequently.

● Puncture stuff: Patches, sandpaper, glue. Anywhere in the world where you see local bikes, you will be able to resupply with puncture repair stuff.

● Spoke key: The ones with plastic handles are the lightest.

● Allen keys: Check which sizes are needed for your bike.

● Cone wrenches: Double-ended cone wrenches can be sawn in half, handles drilled out.

● Chain breaker: The handle can be removed to save weight.

● Adjustable wrench: Miniature model with jaws that extend enough to cater for all nuts on the bike.

● Tyre lever: Normally it is possible to manage with just one (practise before you leave home); the plastic ones are the lightest.

## Bike spares

● Inner tube: Essential as a quick alternative to mending punctures on the trail—use the spare inner tube and repair the puncture at your leisure. A spare is also invaluable in the unlikely event of a complete blow-out that wrecks tyre and tube.

● Spare tyre: Fold so that the diameter is reduced by two-thirds; the tyre will then fit in a pannier or tie to the rack. Most good-quality tyres will last 3,000-6,000 miles (5,000-10,000 kilometers) depending on the proportion of rough surface to tarmac.

● Spokes: Worth taking a few in case a log rips the wheel or a serious buckle begins to cause breakages. Best to start with the best wheels you can afford.

## Expedition recording equipment

● Notebook/pen: Notebooks can be picked up along the route from shops supplying school equipment; pens, too.

● Camera gear: If you need a good-quality record of the expedition, take a 35mm camera body, with fixed lenses (they are lighter and sharper than 'zooms') of, say, 28mm, 50mm, and 150mm. Cameras with mechanical rather than electric shutter releases are said to be more reliable in bad conditions. Film should be carried in the waterproof plastic pots. Spare batteries for the camera should be taken.

## Medical gear

The exact contents of your medical kit depend very much on your destination, and it would be misleading of me to list particular items. But the general areas to cover are: antiseptic (cream or liquid), water purification tablets or iodine, plasters, adhesive tape (can also be used for mending clothes, handlebar tape, etc.), drugs for the country (see your doctor).

## Documents

Again, this depends on your destination, but you should carry in a waterproof bag your maps; passport; driving licence; credit cards; vaccination certificates; letters of introduction; money (cash and travellers' cheques); address list of friends, family, contacts; photos or small presents to give to people who help you along the way.

**Geoff Apps and Range Rider**

# Eccentric Case Studies

There's nothing quite like learning from other people's mistakes, so I have included five of my mountain bike expeditions because they illustrate some of the benefits and pitfalls of planning. They may seem fairly extreme to use as examples—and I'm certainly not commending them as expeditions to be repeated—but I hope they serve as lessons that may help you to cut a few corners.

## 1. The Snowdon Ascent (October 1981)

### What we planned

In 1981 Geoff Apps, a designer then living in Aylesbury, England, was working on the latest version of his homegrown mountain bike—the 'Range Rider'. It was a machine of exquisite workmanship and imaginative design. Steep frame angles and three top tubes gave the bike the looks of a five-bar gate. Motorcycle hub brakes, a bashplate for sliding the bike over rocks and logs, wide bars, and a sprocket-crunching bottom gear of 20.6 inches completed this visionary cycle. Rashly, Geoff allowed me to borrow this valuable one-off for a week.

Snowdon, at 3,560 feet (1,085 meters), is the highest mountain in England and Wales. Like Kilimanjaro, it is unusual in having a weak flank: on its northern side a long ridge provides a gradient so gentle that the Victorians used it to run a tourist railroad to the summit of the mountain. It seemed an obvious place to test the capabilities of Geoff's Range Rider. A team comprising photographer Peter Inglis, Elaine Russell-Wilks, a man with a long beard called 'Rat', and myself, arrived at the bottom of Snowdon at the start of a full-blown autumn gale.

## And what happened

The combination of tyres with tungsten-steel studs and a gears low enough to ride up the bathroom wall gave the bike enough traction to power it up slimy rock-steps and shale that skittered like flakes of ice. The traction was awesome. Too awesome: at around 2,300 feet (700 meters) a loud crunch and a skidding chain announced that two teeth had been ripped off the freewheel. We pressed on with a 34-tooth sprocket reduced to 32 teeth and thighs that were becoming steadily jelly-like. At 2,950 feet (900 meters) the cloud sat down like soggy cotton wool. By the time we reached the ridge above Crib-y-ddysgl, the wind was roaring mightily and visibility was down to a few top tube lengths. Hoisting the bike onto the summit cairn it was a pleasant, if desperately cold, thought that this was probably the first mountain in Britain to be 'mountain biked'.

## The verdict

Apps's bike was an astonishing revelation: it could be ridden in places inconceivable for a normal bicycle. It was only rider tiredness that prevented the Range Rider being ridden the whole way from the bottom to the top of the mountain. With its tight back end and high bottom bracket, this was a bike built to go up very steep hills and over big obstacles; downhill it was heart-stoppingly frisky: hurtling down Snowdon with perhaps a little *too* much gay abandon, Rat lost control and powered straight into a boulder. The front tyre popped, crushed on the rim, and we had to push the bike for the rest of the descent (in the drenching rain we fiddled with numb fingers for 20 minutes and still couldn't get a patch to stick to the wet tube). The lessons were clear: a) mountain bikes are very hard work to pedal uphill—and no less hard to control on the downs; b) 'expedition' riding means carrying spare inner tubes and the tools to make instant repairs; the torque created by ultra-low gears can wreak havoc on a bike's transmission.

# 2. The Fourteen Peaks (June 1984)

## What we planned

British fell-walkers, mountaineers, and runners have for years been setting themselves the target of visiting the summits of all the mountains over 3,000 feet (914 meters) high in North Wales in under 24 hours. They call it the 'Fourteen Peaks'. All the peaks are within the Snowdonia National Park, with the normal starting point being the summit of Snowdon and the finish being the lower rounded summit of Foel-fras. We planned to try it on bikes. The total height gain would be 8,860 feet (2,700 meters) while the total horizontal distance would be 28 miles (45 kilometers), of which 25 miles (40 kilometers) would be off-road. Parts of the route involved mild rock climbing. My companion was my cousin Richard Crane, and our aim was to complete the ride in under twelve hours. To give the ride a worthy climax, we decided to start with the lower, rounded peaks and finish by ascending mighty Snowdon by the knife-edge of the Crib Goch ridge. In planning our exact route we had the benefit of having done the Fourteen Peaks on foot the year before, by the skin of our teeth—in 23½ hours!

The bikes we used were Muddy Fox Pathfinders, standard specification mountain bikes except for the lower gears, which we fitted by swapping the standard freewheel for a SunTour 14-38 block (this gave a bottom gear of 18 inches). Clothing for the day consisted of running shoes, cycling shorts, T-shirts, gloves, and a Goretex jacket each which we tight-rolled onto our handlebars. Each of us had half a Mars Bar taped to the handlebars by the right gear shift lever and we carried two tyre levers, a single spare inner tube and one pump. Our food for the day would be provided by a support team that would meet us first in the Ogwen Valley and then at Pen-y-Pass at the top of Llanberis Pass. The photographer Peter Inglis would act as our guide on the rock climbing sections where micro-terrain route decisions would have vital time implications.

### And what happened

We started up to the first summit at 5.30 a.m., just after dawn. It was a perfect day: clear skies and a sun that brought a sparkle to the lakes. Much of the route was ridable, with some notable exceptions. On the ascent of Bristly Ridge we overtook two rock-climbers who later told us they had nearly fallen off when two cyclists had clambered past them using bicycles as gigantic 'chocks' to climb a chimney. The whole ride went like clockwork—except that we finished outside our target time, in 12 hours 26 minutes.

### The verdict

Although neither of us was seriously injured, this is not a ride to be repeated—especially as Snowdonia is now under such visitor pressure that mountain bikers must look to lesser populated parts of these spectacular mountains. It was, however, the Fourteen Peaks that told Richard and I what we needed to know for 'Bicycles up Kilimanjaro'. Later, we attempted the English equivalent of the Fourteen Peaks: the four mountains over 3,000 feet (914 meters) in England are all in the Lake District. It was the beginning of winter and we fought through gales of wind and rain, a puncture and then darkness to ride over Skiddaw, Scafell Pike, Sca Fell, and Helvellyn in 16 hours 2 minutes. It was HORRIBLE!

## 3. The Ridgeway by Night (November 1985)
### What we planned

There is in southern England a hill track that has been used since the Stone Age. It runs from the River Thames at Streatley, just west of London, to the massive stone circle at Avebury in Wiltshire. The track climbs and falls for 37 glorious miles (60 kilometers) through Wessex, the ancient Anglo-Saxon kingdom established by Prince Cerdic and his son Cynric in about 495 AD. In 1984 I had mountain biked the Ridgeway by day, taking 12 hours to amble along beneath a skylarked summer ceiling. Mostly the surface is rough chalk impregnated with razor sharp flints, interspersed with sections of turf well chewed by horses' hooves. Near the western end there is a 5-mile (8-kilometer) section of road. Attempting a night ride along the Ridgeway would be an interesting variation on a theme. And more interesting still would be to try it in

**Bicycles up Kilimanjaro: Dress for . . .**

midwinter. To give ourselves a time challenge we aimed to be standing in the centre of the stone circle at Avebury to see the dawn.

The team for this attempt comprised myself and cousins Adrian and Richard Crane. We equipped ourselves with three Renegade mountain bikes and Petzl head flashlights (the theory being that on rough terrain in the dark it's easier to ride if the light beam follows your eyes rather than the bike handlebars). We had chosen our night ride to coincide with a full moon. We carried with us some chocolate bars and strapped to the underneath of each saddle a pair of Goretex pants and a tool kit. We each wore a Goretex mountain climber's jacket, mittens, and woolly hats. At approximately one-third distance we would rendezvous with our support crew, John Nixon, who would feed us quickly before we pressed on.

## And what happened

As the town clocks chimed 10 p.m. we pedalled from Streatley into the starry night. Already the temperature was below freezing. Initially, the going was easy: the pale chalk track shone in the moonlight and we reached our rendezvous with John Nixon around midnight. It took a few minutes to gulp hot soup and then we plunged again into the darkness. Into the small hours the temperature continued to fall and our tyres crackled through frozen puddles. Past the great White Horse of Uffington, the Iron Age castle, and the old tomb called Wayland's Smithy we bounced. Then it began to snow, softening flakes driven on a hard wind. In a confusion of tracks near Ogbourne St George we became lost, and powering along a field edge, a branch from a fallen tree scythed into my rear wheel and neatly folded the derailleur into a ball of crumpled aluminium. Adrian, a past master at emergency bodges, bent the mechanism straight with his hands so that the chain would at least run over one sprocket. We slowed

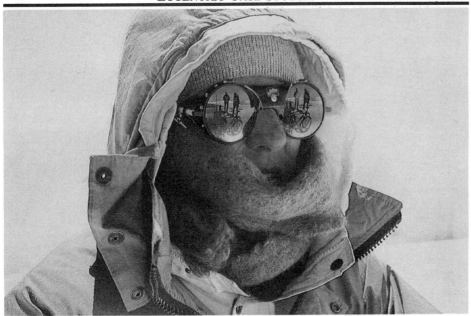

. . . **changing conditions**

down, the ice turning to mud. As the sky lightened we still had several miles to go. Mud and leaves were now jamming the wheels in the frame; stopping at a farmyard we borrowed a hose and blasted the bikes clean before wheeling on and down to Avebury. Around breakfast time we rolled, muddy and tired, into the stone circle.

## The verdict

Night riding on mountain bikes is one of *the* great adventures. For safety's sake you have to choose well-defined tracks that are not bedevilled by boulders, or visited by precipices over which you could pedal in the dark. So bright was the moon on our ride, and so reflective was the white chalk track, that we did not use the head flashlights for riding, though they were handy for reading the map. Obviously the best conditions are a dry moonlit night. The winter condition added to the 'other-dimensional' aspect of our ride, the frozen fields and trees contributing to the utter still of the dead of night. Riding in the dark produced two cautionary incidents: early in the ride our only map dropped out of my pocket and disappeared into the night for good—and then the unseen branch wrecked my gears. I blame both these incidents on the peculiar difficulties of riding bicycles semi-sightless; Dick and Adrian attributed the accidents to a more prosaic cause! Overall we found the darkness cut by half the average speed you would expect to travel over rough ground by mountain bike.

# 4. Bicycles up Kilimanjaro (December 1984-January 1985)

## What we planned

The idea was to ride bicycles up the highest mountain in Africa to raise money for the London-based charity Intermediate Technology. The plan was hatched with my

**En route to the Centre of the Earth: maps and roads often failed
to match.**

cousin Richard Crane. Kilimanjaro is 19,340 feet (5,894 meters) high; a volcano which
is snow-capped in winter, set on the equator on the border between Kenya and Tanzania.
We had been looking for a mountain with a gentle enough gradient to allow us to
ride the bikes for as much of the ascent as possible. Kilimanjaro is ideal: of all the
world's big mountains, Kilimanjaro is unique for the gentleness of its lower slopes;
having talked to Dick's sister Bar (who had climbed the mountain already), it seemed
likely that we would be able to ride to a height of 15,500 feet (4,724 meters), where
we would meet the final cinder cone of the volcano and have to carry the bikes for
a steep 3,000 feet (914 meters). The final part of the ascent would be on snow and
ice, following a precarious route around the rim of the volcano to the summit at Uhuru
Peak.

Timing for the ride was critical to our fund raising effort. Intermediate Technology
helps people work themselves out of poverty, and one of their many projects that
year was the installation of a wind pump in the semi-desert of north-east Kenya, which
would lift water from an underground reservoir to a TB hospital. Our goal was to
raise the $20,000 or so needed to buy and install the wind pump. To raise the money
we needed publicity, and the *The Sunday Times* generously offered to give us front

page treatment if we could relay the story and photos from the slopes of Kilimanjaro in time to meet their deadlines.

So eager were we to make the press deadlines that we left no contingency uncovered. Richard and I would ride the bicycles; Peter Inglis would take photographs (travelling by mountain bike then by foot); Michèle Young, Catriona Hall, and Maggie Birkhead would act as relay runners to rush copy and photos down the mountain to the stringer from *The Sunday Times*, who would then dash to Nairobi and the plane for London. Michèle, Kate, and Maggie would also coordinate our supplies and porters. The assembled tents, paraffin stoves, fuel, high altitude clothing, ice axes, a rope, crampons, dehydrated soup, sleeping bags, and a small furry teddy bear from my father Hol—and three Saracen mountain bikes—weighed 286 lb. (130 kg.)!

## And what happened

The early miles, through dense jungle dripping with morning storms, were a hilarious splatter of mud and fun. The third bike was ditched by Peter within hours of starting; he found it easier to walk! By the evening of the third day we were at Kibo Hut, poised below the final volcanic cone for a summit push. Our porters declined the invitation to continue beyond this point and we carried the bikes and packs containing tent, sleeping gear, food and stove in one long, breathless slog, to the crater rim 3,000 feet (914 meters) above, then returned to collect the packs containing our personal gear and climbing equipment. At 3 a.m. on the fifth day, all six of us, plus Nicas our guide, set off from Kibo Hut, climbing back up to our dump of the day before. Here Nicas left us, and we cached the tent and supplies, setting off for Uhuru Peak with the two bikes and a pack each containing emergency clothing and supplies. Since we were moving on hard frozen snow and ice, we took with us the rope, ice axes and crampons. The riding was exhilarating; exhausting. In the thin air at 19,000 feet (5,790 meters) breath came in stabbing gasps. We reached the summit at 2 p.m. on New Year's Eve, gathering in a happy group of six for photographs, before beginning the freewheel of a lifetime.

## The verdict

'Bicycles up Kilimanjaro' made the front page of *The Sunday Times*—and many other papers, too. In the following months £27,500 was donated by the public to Intermediate Technology; enough to buy not one, but three wind pumps. We recovered the cost of the expedition (about £4,000) through writing magazine articles and selling photographs. As an adventure it was a delightful mixture of thrill and absurdity—with a little danger thrown in for good measure. The mountain bikes did not suffer any punctures or breakdowns, and though heavy by today's standards, they performed well. Our main lesson was that, while it was great fun to learn about co-ordinating all the personnel and equipment of a full-blown expedition, the sledgehammer tactics created a monster so cumbersome that some items of equipment were not seen for days on end! In future, it seemed better to follow Intermediate Technology's motto: 'Small is Beautiful'.

**To the Centre of the Earth: somewhere in Tibet with 2,000 miles to go.**

# 5. Journey to the Centre of the Earth
# (May-June 1986)

## What we planned

Again the idea was to raise money for Intermediate Technology by taking on a challenge that was both difficult and one which had not been done before. The team was Richard and myself, and we planned to cycle to the place in the world most distant from the open sea. It seemed that nobody had either pinpointed this spot or visited it. Using formulae devised for mariners we found the 'Centre of the Earth' to be in the far north-west of the Gobi desert. It seemed suitably inaccessible to merit an attempt to reach it by bicycle. We chose to start our ride at the open sea, on the Bay of Bengal. We reckoned the overall distance to be in the region of 3,100 miles (5,000 kilometers), and the main difficulties to be the crossing of the Tibetan plateau (which had not been crossed by bicycle before) and then the crossing of the Gobi desert (which, again, we could find no record of having been cycled before). After looking at the climate charts for central Asia it became clear that we would only have a short window in the weather during which to make our ride: we dare not start before the end of April because the passes over the Himalayas and Tibet would still be blocked by snow, yet if we left it too late, or cycled too slowly, we would arrive at the Gobi desert at the hottest time of year. Even if we managed the ride in fifty days, the desert temperatures would already be creeping over 105°F by late June.

Unlike previous jaunts, we put a fair bit of research into choosing the right bicycles for the job (see Hardware section). To travel fast meant an absolute minimum of luggage, mounted on bikes that could be sprinted on tarmac and powered through snow and sand. By the time every item had been pared down to the last molecule, the bikes weighed 22 lb. and all our luggage and clothes weighed 18 lb.

## And what happened

We started from a beach in Bangladesh at noon on May 1, 1986, pedalling up through the Ganges Delta and into India. During these early days we were speeding along on proper roads, notching our longest day (149 miles (240 kilometers)) across the flat frying pan plain of Bihar State. Through Nepal life got harder: landslides blocked the road, we were buffeted by the early monsoon and slaved up 95 miles (153 kilometers) and 15,090 feet (4,600 meters) of continual climbing through the border to our first Tibetan pass, the 17,106-foot (5,214-meter) Lalung Le. The road to Lhasa was dirt for all but the last few hours: for over 400 miles (700 kilometers) the bikes bucked and bounced and half-way we modified our pannier attachments so that the bags were held tight to the rack by a single up-and-over strap. At night we slept in tented road camps, truckers' halts, with Tibetan horsemen, in caves and in mountain gullies. Overhead a riven sky half a world wide alternately spat snow and shone like a bursting bomb. Our daily halts in nomads' tents and lonely work camps were agonizingly cosy respites during which we would hug mugs of salt tea and force down handfuls of tsampa watched by the kindest eyes any traveller could ever hope to meet. The ride north from Lhasa across the Tibetan plateau was hard: 1,048 miles (1,686 kilometers) and three passes of over 16,400 feet (5,000 meters). One of the few consolations during these wild days was a downhill section that lasted 114 miles (183 kilometers)! The final section of the ride, 761 miles (1,224 kilometers) through the Gobi desert was meant to be our finishing sprint, but somebody had forgotten to surface the road and for over three hundred miles we had to fight the bikes over anything from massive tyre ruts to soft gravel that sucked us to a standstill. At 8.10 p.m. on the 58th day we reached the Centre of the Earth—a shallow bowl of small dead desert shrubs set in several million acres of sand.

## The verdict

Journey to the Centre of the Earth was a ride so big, fast, and continually hard that it's difficult to imagine I'll manage another ride like it! The bicycles were remarkable: two punctures each during the whole 3,286 miles (5,301 kilometers)—of which about a quarter were on dirt roads—and only one breakage, a gear cable. This was fortunate because our only spares were six spokes, one inner tube, two tires (which we did not need), and a washer for the pump.

# 6. The Northwest Quadrant
## (Coming next)

I'm always slightly awed by travellers who come up with an instant, believable response to the most common question of all, 'What are you going to do next?' I normally have to invent a journey on the spur of the moment, and usually I come out with something daft and slightly facetious like: 'I'm going cave-biking.'

But for once in my life I do have a well-advanced plan: Bicycles up Olympus Mons, BOM for short. Olympus Mons is a real place. It's the most magnificent of the Tharsis group of volcanoes, 78,000 feet high and crowned by a caldera 40 miles wide. It is in these dimensions that the attraction lies: Olympus Mons is the largest volcano known to man, and as such has a 'tag' ideally suited to the promotional hype so necessary for the success of a twentieth century bicycle expedition. Another motive is that in 1984, my cousin Richard and I were credited in *The Guinness Book of Records* with having set a new height record for cycling: 19,340 feet. Since then, Dick's brother Adrian went higher when he took a mountain bike up Mount Chimborazo in South America. Riding Olympus Mons should keep me ahead for years—light years in fact.

The logistics for BOM are well advanced. The most costly element in this expedition is the journey out to the mountain, which is 292,000,000 miles from London. In the northwest quadrant of the planet Mars to be imprecise.

After the ascent of Olympus Mons there should be time to try the descent into Vallis

Marineris, a valley 20,000 feet deep and 2,500 miles long. But then Mars is perfect mountain bike terrain; a dramatic combination of gigantic volcanoes, rubble-strewn deserts, bottomless canyons, dust storms, ice caps, and an atmosphere that is 95 per cent carbon dioxide. It should just about make it sufficiently attractive to off-road enthusiasts seeking a suitably hostile environment—and one that should be declared an area of outstanding natural deadness as soon as possible!

# Index